Michael

THE DOMESTIC REVOLUTION

The Domestic Revolution

*The Modernisation of Household Service
in England and France 1820-1920*

THERESA M. McBRIDE

CROOM HELM LONDON

First published 1976
Copyright © 1976 by Theresa M. McBride

Croom Helm Ltd, 2-10 St John's Road, London SW11

ISBN 0-85664-220-7

Printed in Great Britain by Biddles of Guildford

CONTENTS

LIST OF ILLUSTRATIONS AND TABLES

ACKNOWLEDGEMENTS

My greatest debt is to Peter N. Stearns whose critical judgement and editorial expertise have been invaluable. I can only begin to fully express my gratitude for his considerable assistance. I am also grateful to Patricia Branca, David Chaplin, and Leonore Davidoff, who made their own work available to me and made important suggestions for the design of the book.

Financial support for this project was provided at various stages by Rutgers University, the National Endowment for the Humanities, and above all, by Holy Cross College through the Batchelor Fellowship Program.

Strawberry Hill Farm   Theresa M. McBride
May 1975.

FOR MY PARENTS

INTRODUCTION

Of all the major social groups in modern European history, the most completely ignored has been the servant class.[1] Historians have been content to take servants for granted in the same way that their employers expected them to be always unobtrusively present. The decline in servants early in the twentieth century in Europe and the United States led to the almost total disappearance of the servant from the middle-class home and thereby to the loss of interest in writing about servants at any level. The ubiquitous servant of the nineteenth century deserves a better fate.

The reasons for the neglect are not hard to find. The servant has not interested the social or labour historian concerned with class struggle since servants did not form a true social class. Although recognised by law as a distinctive social group, servants did not have a class identity, since for most domestics, household employment was not a permanent occupation. The most important fact about domestic service in the nineteenth century was that service was merely a temporary though often crucial stage in an individual's life. Moreover, servants were isolated from the mainstream of working-class activities and aspirations, and contributed nothing to the nineteenth-century struggle of labour for recognition. Working alone or with only one or two other domestics in a middle- or upper-class household, the servant gained no sense of class solidarity and the great majority remained politically inactive.

Another reason for the neglect is perhaps the fact that the majority of nineteenth-century servants were female. One of the characteristic aspects of domestic service after 1800 was the feminisation of service — the balance between males and females in service was increasingly tipped toward the women so that by the First World War service was substantially a female occupation. Demographers, to whom servants might appeal because of their geographical mobility, have been much more concerned with male migration and have almost totally overlooked the marked venturesomeness of the female servant and the contribution of service to the formation of modern urban populations. Social and economic historians have ignored servants because they performed what was traditionally women's work which lay outside the most obvious urban economic activities and had no 'exchange' value. As a traditional framework for women, servants performed services which had no standard economic valuation. Until these services can be fully commercialised and performed outside the home, domestic service will continue to remain outside the realm of measurable urban economic activities. Already in a dependent economic position by the fact of being a woman, the female servant's position *vis-à-vis* economic and social activity was considered unremarkable.

Finally, servants did not leave a large body of literature which could serve to elucidate the conditions of their work, their aspirations, and their relationships with their employers. Like most groups in the popular classes, what is known of servants is largely derived from their employers' accounts of them. This fact introduces some significant stumbling-blocks into the study of servants and leaves us with a picture of the servant not as a historical person but as a 'problem.'

The scant historical writing that has dealt with the servants has focused on two aspects of domestic service: the relationship between the servant and the middle classes in the nineteenth century and the connection of domestic service to urban migration patterns. Historians of the middle class have concerned themselves with servants only to the degree that the servant can be used to define the middle class. Adeline Daumard and Louis Chevalier in their studies of the social topography of Paris have argued for the usefulness of the number of servants in defining the social character of the different quarters.[2] J. A. Banks has insisted that the inclination to employ servants was an essential characteristic of the middle-class mentality in Victorian England.[3] Indeed, J. F. C. Harrison has argued that 'a growing demand for personal service was one of the earliest signs of middle-class prosperity',[4] and that servant employment 'played an essential part in defining' the middle class.[5] However, this identification of the servant with the middle class may be misleading. The extent to which servants were shaped by their association with the middle class or even consciously educated by their masters in middle-class values needs to be examined, but this is a subject to which historians of the middle class have added little.

Although the importance of domestic service for feminine urban migration has been recognised, the distinctive qualities of both male and female servant migration have not been explored in spite of their divergence from the conventional patterns of male labour migration. Domestic positions absorbed the majority of single females who migrated to the cities and also a significant segment of the male migrants.[6] Why rural emigrants came to the cities and what they hoped to find are questions to which the study of domestics can suggest answers. Service removed the worries of seeking food and shelter in the city and offered a base from which the servant could seek other work. The role of domestic service was thus a traditionally important channel for urban migration and assimilation, which peaked in importance during the greatest wave of urban migration between 1820 and 1856.[7] The process of assimilation was slow and at times incomplete, as in France for example, where many servants retained strong ties with the countryside from which they had come, sometimes returning there to marry or to retire. Nevertheless, domestic service constituted the transition for many young men and women from rural to urban life in the eighteenth and nineteenth centuries and it declined when the need for this channel was beginning to disappear.

Finally, domestic service has played a pivotal role in the modernisation of women which needs to be explored. It is clear that for women the process of modernisation involved the existence of work outside their homes. This does not mean that women who continued to work only within the household were not modernised, but that for women as a group, modernisation came largely as a result of the broadening of roles for women outside of the traditional familial ones. Thus, it is not surprising that historians interested in the question of women's evolving role in society have tended to focus upon working women. What is surprising is that historians of women have ignored the largest occupational category of women outside of agriculture — domestic service.

This study of domestic servants, then, seeks to answer the questions posed by historians of the middle class and of women and by studies of urban migration, but it must also go further in investigating the servants themselves, where they came from and what they did as servants. The term 'servant' itself needs definition because the words 'domestique' and 'servant' were applied to a wide variety of occupations in the nineteenth century. Strictly speaking, a servant was one who occupied himself exclusively with the personal needs of an employer and of his family in such a way that this occupation established a relationship of personal dependence on the employer. The cultural ideal was a household servant who would be lodged and fed by the employer. However, both in common usage and for the official purposes of the census, the terms denoted equally a household employee and a hired agricultural worker, and they often failed to distinguish between those who lived in and those who did not. This study is solely concerned with the household servant in urban areas and with some of the 'domestics' who did not live in, such as married male servants and charwomen; the servants of agricultural families have been excluded to avoid ambiguity.[8]

Who were the individuals whose work placed them in this general category of domestics? The men were mainly valets, footmen (the French termed them 'valets de chambre' and 'valets de pied'), and coachmen. The former was the personal servant of his master, responsible for caring for the personal effects of his employer. In larger households, there might be a variety of valets or footmen with specialised duties: care of the silver and fine china, help in serving meals, and so forth. Valets were the largest category of male domestics. The coachman's primary responsibility was obvious, but he occasionally also served in a general capacity in smaller households. Many English households were overseen by a butler, but the French equivalent, known as an 'intendant' or 'steward', was much rarer. In France only a very large country household or one with extensive landholdings listed a steward among their servants. Urban households in both France and

England were more often placed in the care of a female housekeeper or cook-housekeeper.

Women servants were much more numerous and their titles and responsibilities were more diverse. The most descriptive title and the position of widest responsibility was the 'maid-of-all-work' ('bonne à tout faire'). This title became increasingly used toward the end of the century as household staffs declined in size. Roughly two-thirds of all female domestics were general servants, whose responsibilities were broad and unspecified. Chambermaids and cooks were much less numerous than maids-of-all-work and their wages were correspondingly greater, indicating a higher level of status within the servant hierarchy. In the French household, the chambermaid was the mistress's personal maid, keeping her clothing in order and in good repair, arranging her mistress's hair, helping her dress and so forth, and also being responsible for cleaning some rooms and for serving meals. In wealthy English households, a 'lady's maid' was employed for this purpose. The cook, who was generally a female when employed in a private home, was responsible for shopping for provisions, cooking, and superintending in the kitchen. In larger households, the cook received the assistance of a young girl employed for this purpose, known as an 'aide de cuisine', 'kitchen maid', or 'scullery maid' for whom this was a domestic apprenticeship, and who performed the heaviest domestic tasks.[9] In moderately-sized staffs, the cook and housekeeper were the same servant, and she aided in engaging all the lower servants.[10]

Those who could afford a large staff of servants sometimes employed a specialised group of servants who were charged with the care of the children. First was the wet nurse whose sole function was the nursing of the newborn child, and who was employed for a limited period, such as six months. The nurse's position among the other servants was somewhat ambiguous since she sometimes merited special privileges.[11] But in France most wet nurses did not become members of the employer's household but had the children brought to their own homes.[12] English households employed fewer wet nurses than did the French, but in England the term 'nurse' applied also to the individual who cared for the mother for a short period of post-partum recovery.[13] This 'monthly nurse' was a different servant from the wet nurse, but the use of the same term to apply to both tends to confuse their functions. To care for children after weaning, there was a nursery maid or 'bonne d'enfant'. Finally, in the wealthiest households, children were cared for by a governess or instructress. The instructress's title in France implied a level of education which placed her above the servant class to which the nursery maid and even the governess belonged.[14] In England, the status of the governess was more ambiguous. Since some governesses were recruited from among the daughters of middle-class and professional men, governesses were often not considered to be servants.[15] But not all governesses were the impoverished gentlewomen of popular imagery who sought such jobs as a means of preserving genteel status.

In addition, there were several categories of household personnel whose titles put them on the margins of the servant group. The most important numerically were the 'femmes de ménage' and charwomen. Strictly speaking, the 'femme de ménage' or charwoman was a 'daily', hired by the day and not lodged by her employer.[16] Although usually considered a domestic servant, the charwoman will be discussed separately whenever possible since she did not belong to the class of live-in servants. Another confusing term which appears rather frequently in nineteenth-century French sources was the 'femme de confiance'. This title commonly applied to a servant who was a kind of housekeeper, responsible for the household in general and for directing the other servants.[17]

Finally, there was the lady's companion or 'dame de compagnie', whose position was superior to that of most domestics but whose relationship to her mistress was a dependent one, and who was not a member of the domestic servant class. Excluding the wet nurses who worked in their own homes and the 'femmes de ménage' and charwomen, this whole group of women involved in child care and household direction from nursery maids to ladies' companions, numbered only about one-tenth of the whole servant class. There were other occupations, however, which should not be classed as household servants but which were often included among the domestic occupations. 'Concierges', 'portiers', 'gatekeepers', and 'lodgekeepers' were classified as servants in the censuses for lack of a more appropriate category but they deserve a specific classification of their own. Except in rare cases, the French *concierge* was an employee in a large apartment building rather than the servant of an individual employer. Similarly, gatekeepers, groundskeepers and gardeners were separately housed so that they were more independent than the servants who worked in the house. Moreover, this group of servants were more often found in country houses than in urban households, and consequently they have been excluded here from the category of urban domestic servants.[18]

At a very different social level which was numerically very important, nearly every butcher and baker employed a 'domestic' in the nineteenth-century city, yet no distinction was made between a girl who served the baker and his family and the one who worked as a clerk in a bakery or cheese shop. It is possible that the hired girl performed both functions but the ambiguity of the case illustrates very well the problems of defining the limits of the servant class.

Despite the difficulties of definition and even taking the narrowly-defined urban domestic servant group, servants comprised an important segment of the urban population in the nineteenth century. The French census of 1861 gave the total number of servants in Paris as 111,496, or 6.1 percent of the total urban population.[19] The servant percentage of the total population continued to increase until the number of servants in Paris reached a peak in 1896 of 7.9 per cent and then began to decline.[20] In 1886, there was an average of 216 servants for every 1,000 French households.[21] Since some households included two or more servants, about one French family in six had a servant between 1830 and 1880.[22] In terms of the servants themselves, the experience of servanthood was very common: in 1866, domestics throughout France comprised 29 per cent of the active female population, while in 1901 they constituted nearly 45 per cent of all working women in Paris.[23]

The experience of working as a servant was even more important in England: in 1861 in London, one in every three women between the ages of 15 and 24 was a servant, and better than one in every six women (10 to 95) was listed as a domestic.[24] Throughout most of the nineteenth century, the total number of servants (both male and female) in England and Wales increased, from 908,138 in 1851 to 1,549,502 in 1891, and then began to decline only in percentage terms but without significantly diminishing the servant class until 1921.[25] Thus, the English and French patterns follow a generally similar path in the course of the nineteenth century, although the French servant population kept better pace with the general population increase than did that of England, and peaked earlier.

As case studies of nineteenth-century domestic service, England and France serve the comparative purposes of this book very well since their patterns of economic growth and urbanisation differed, and yet domestic service played an important role in the social development of both countries in the nineteenth century. This does not mean that the patterns of the development of domestic service in these two countries were unique. The history of domestic service in nineteenth-century Europe and the United States is broadly similar to the pattern that will be described for France and England. Indeed, recent studies of the evolution of some Latin American societies indicate that domestic service is 'clearly *the major setting for female urban labour force participation during the transitional stages of industrialisation.*'[26] Hence, the history of domestic service has more to do with stages of economic development than with particular cultural styles.[27]

In England and in France, the 'Dual' Revolution (French and Industrial) assured the triumph of the middle-class way of life of which a typical assertion was the employment of a servant. The number of domestic servants peaked in the middle of the nineteenth century and in that period the most important impact of service on urban migration was felt. Although this study begins in the 1820s with the publication of the first domestic economy manuals, the trend toward an increasing number of urban domestic servants and their spread into middle-class homes had already become apparent at least fifty years before. Again the early stages of modernisation and domestic service went hand in hand.

14

More superficially, the turn of the century did clarify the legal definition and status of the French servant class. In the initial stages of the Revolution of 1789, some servants had become involved in political activities, such as the demonstrations of August 1789, in which servants demanded full citizenship,[28] and others had been led to violence against their former masters,[29] earning them a reputation for rebelliousness. While establishing legal equality for all French citizens, the constitutions of the revolutionary era suspended all political rights of those who served as domestics.[30] The Napoleonic Code refused to recognise the independent status of the servant, considering a domestic to be too dependent on his master to be recognised as a civil person.[31] In England, no new formal legislation was passed, and the servant continued to be defined throughout the nineteenth century as the dependent of his or her employer. Servants and women were the last groups in the society to be enfranchised in both France and England.[32] Consequently, the nineteenth-century domestic servant had the same status in the eyes of the law as a child, protected by and subject to the authority of the parent/employer.

A more novel legacy of the revolutionary era in England as well as in France was the decline in the number of men in service.[33] In the French case this was undoubtedly due in the short run to the involvement of some male servants in revolutionary activity and to the need for men in the military forces after 1792. England faced similar pressures on manpower as her involvement in war deepened. Basically, however, the decline in male servants marked the change from aristocratic employment to middle-class employment and set forth the nineteenth-century pattern of the feminisation of domestic service.

The early nineteenth century was an era of tremendous urban growth in both England and France, with the strongest period of growth falling between 1820 and 1856, after which urban expansion slowed.[34] This period also saw the expansion of the urban middle class as the leading employers of servants. This development was signalled by the publication of a great number of manuals on servants and on domestic economy generally. The first of these manuals was published in France in 1821,[35] but many others were printed in both France and England in succeeding years. The unprecedented proliferation of manuals in the nineteenth century reflected the need for assistance in coping with the increasing complexities of domestic life by the women of the new middle classes who were newly facing the problems of dealing with servants.[36]

This study ends with the First World War in order to take full advantage of the awakening of interest in the problem of the decline of servants, and more important, in the fact of this decline. The 1910s marked the end of the period in which domestic service was an integral part of the middle-class way of life. The war economy struck a final blow to the institution of live-in service because the improved employment market attracted young women away from domestic service by the higher salaries and the greater freedom in other occupations.[37] The pattern of decline was already established in the 1880s, but the upheaval of the war accelerated the trend and was in that sense the end of an era.

Modern servanthood, as exemplified in France and England, proved to be a roughly century-long transition which caused the middle class and a large number of servants to come to grips with change. In this sense, the occupation was unique — not the direct forerunner of contemporary life but a way-station which affected millions of people and, even fifty years after the end of the transition, its marks are still clearly visible on both middle-class and working-class society.

The rise and fall of domestic service between the Napoleonic age and the First World War is a key to the modernisation process — a process which commonly involves a dialectic of concurrent change and resistance to that change. Nineteenth-century writings on servants illuminate an important facet of that dialectic — the way in which change was perceived as compared to the actual changes. This study includes an analysis of contemporary reflections of the servant problem to the degree that they may convey the perceptions of servant-employers of the changes that were occurring. The new group of servant-employers in the nineteenth century believed that their problems with servants were novel and they viewed the nineteenth-century situation as a deterioration from the Old Régime. In France, there arose the misconception that the French Revolution had destroyed the family life of the Old Régime, in which servants had been associate members. The classic French statement of this view was that of Frédéric Le Play.

> The apprentice-servant was then completely assimilated into a member of the family; he was treated like the other children of the family and made friendships with them which survived this temporary cohabitation. He identified himself with all the sentiments and interests of the family. He remained all his life attached to that household.[38]

English employers and commentators were no less concerned with the changing nature of the master-servant relationship. Correctly or not, they often insisted that the servants of the eighteenth century had been more attached to their employers, more loyal, and more willing to accept their proper 'place' in society.[39] This theme of the eighteenth-century servant as a model of loyalty reflected their deep sense of dissatisfaction with the nineteenth-century servant situation, but its implication of a total shift in the problems was unjustified. The nineteenth century did not introduce the problems which will be described in this study, but the problems were intensified by the new urban concentrations of domestic service.

Although nineteenth-century employers were thus often mistaken in their perception of the evolving character of domestic service, they were not incorrect in recognising the importance of the changes. The nineteenth century was a crucial period of transition, and domestic service had a vital role to play in the modernisation process. Servanthood, as will be explored in succeeding chapters, was the chief means by which large numbers of people effected the transition to modern urban society. Ironically, the decline of domestic service was the final result of that transition.

1. THE MIDDLE-CLASS HOUSEHOLD

After 1800 the young doctor starting his practice or the new wife of a factory manager when setting up a house thought first of hiring a servant. This was a characteristic expectation in middle-class life during the nineteenth century. Historians of the French and English middle classes, despite their profound arguments over the nature of this segment of society, agree that the most distinctive expenditure of the middle-class budget was the employment of a servant. This relationship was so unique that Adeline Daumard in her definition of the French middle class argued that 'Middle-class life can scarcely be conceived without the servants. To know the number of families served by domestics allows one to as exactly evaluate the number of middle-class families.'[1] This is also a commonplace in British social history in the same period. J. A. Banks confirmed the criterion in his study of the Victorian middle class; he commented that the middle-class outlook was one in which the keeping of servants played a major part.[2] Servants were a status symbol and to lack domestic help in a middle-class household, argued one historian, was to risk sinking 'from genteel poverty . . . into the darkness of vulgarity.'[3] 'I must not do our household work, or carry my baby out: or I should lose caste,' insisted the wife of an English assistant surgeon in 1859. 'We must keep a servant.'[4] Hence, it was the location of servants within an urban population that defined the social topography according to Louis Chevalier: 'in Paris especially . . . it is the mass of servants much more than the middle class which politically and socially differentiates the sections of the city.'[5]

An illustration of what this meant for the middle-class life-style can be found in a comparison of the employment of servants by two men of disparate social and economic position in Lyons in 1872. The Director of the Banque de France, Blandin, his wife and three children were served by two live-in domestics: a female cook and a valet. A cashier at the same bank named Auger and his wife also employed a female servant although they had no children.[6] Considering the relative size of the two families and the disparity in their social positions, the distinction in the number of servants is minor. This case illustrates how the employment of servants helped to define the distinctiveness of the entire middle class despite tremendous disparity in income levels and social status.

Throughout the nineteenth century, the significance of the servant's relationship to the middle-class way of life was profound. For its part, domestic service acquired a different character and expanded to play an

18

important role in the evolution of urban society. During the first part
of the nineteenth century the middle classes in France and England
expanded rapidly (in France in 1820 this class constituted about
15 per cent of the urban population).[7] The middle classes were
'transformed, renewed, and enlarged' by an influx of new people.[8]
In England, the number of people who fell into the middle income
bracket of £200 to £500 per year doubled between 1851 and 1871,
while total population increased only 11.9 percent by 1861 and
13.2 per cent by 1871.[9] These new men from modest rural families
had worked their way up to become the heads or managers of
commercial and industrial enterprises. They now created a great
demand for household servants as the symbol of and the reward for
their success, and perhaps as a necessity for the kind of functions they
expected from their wives as well. For, contrary to some impressions, it
was the wives who generally dealt with servants and who felt the most
direct need for them. The expanding number of positions for servants
in middle-class homes accompanied an influx of new servants, most of
them recent immigrants from the surrounding farmlands.[10] This
expansion of the servant and employer classes inevitably raised the
level of friction in master-servant relationships, because of the newness
of both groups to their positions. The 'servant problem' became such a
critical one for the middle classes that one commentator suggested that
the selection of a servant was as important for the *petit bourgeois* wife
as the choice of a husband.[11] More seriously, authors of household
economy manuals warned that 'the question of domestics is one of such
importance in a household that one cannot overestimate it,'[12] and that
'without a single exception, servants are the greatest plague connected
with housekeeping.'[13]

Increasing middle-class employment of servants in the nineteenth
century set the pattern of the family served by a single maid-of-all-work,
whereas the few sources on eighteenth-century society which discuss
servants described aristocratic staffs as typically large.[14] It is probable
that poorer aristocrats no less than most middle-class families in the
eighteenth century employed few servants or none at all and by the
nineteenth century, aristocratic households were not always exceptional
in comparison to middle-class household size. The household of French
aristocratic landowner Francois de Neufchâteau, for example, was
served by three to four domestics between 1815 and 1827.[15] Larger
household staffs continued to be employed in English country houses[16]
and among the very rich throughout the nineteenth century, but the
urban middle and upper classes were spreading the supply of domestic
help ever more thinly among the growing number of servant-employing
households.

For despite the descriptions in domestic economy manuals of
extensive household staffs and elaborate servant hierarchies, the
average servant-employing household in the nineteenth century included

only one or two servants. An analysis of the population in Versailles in 1872, for example, revealed that of the 410 male servants and 2,211 female domestics, 80 per cent worked alone in a family or with only one other servant.[17] Slightly more than half of the servants (1,348) were the only domestics in the household where they served, making the 'typical' servant the one who worked alone. The figures for servants working in Lyons in the same year are even more striking. There were 9,517 female servants and 1,010 males, out of which only 3,179 worked in households where more than one servant was employed.[18] Thus, 70 per cent of the servants in Lyons in 1872 worked alone. Hence, the image of the French middle-class household which could not function without the services of a cook, a chambermaid, and either a third female servant or a coachman-valet was obviously not founded in fact.[19]

A similarly false image of large household staffs for middle-class families is even more pervasive in English history. The English historians' insistence that a middle-class household was incomplete without its three servants[20] is based on the evidence of the English domestic economy manuals where 'the emphasis was laid upon the number of servants ought to be kept, but it was always taken for granted that some, or at least one, were essential to middle-class well-being.'[21] One of these manuals published about 1845 argued that even an income of £100 per year was sufficient to employ a single maid-of-all-work,[22] although other manuals, including Mrs Beeton's very successful *Book of Household Management* (1861), set the minimum limit for servants at an income of £150 to £200 per year.[23] Only after achieving an income of £300 or more could a family afford to introduce a second servant into the household.[24] Since the bulk of the middle class in mid-nineteenth-century England earned less than £300 per year,[25] only a small minority of middle-class families could afford more than a single servant. A Labour Department study of London's households in 1894 found that 27 per cent of the servant-employing households had only one servant and 35 per cent more had only two.[26] Samplings of the London census lists from 1851 and 1871 found 34 per cent of the servant-employing households with only one servant and 25 per cent with two.[27] And neither of these studies touches the middle-class housewife who, even with the careful budgeting urged by the manuals, was unable to afford even a single maid-of-all-work.

In fact, the attempt to define the middle class by the employment of even one servant is not completely accurate. Not every family which can be defined as middle-class by occupational and income-level criteria employed a servant. This criterion is not met by all of the professionals in France, whose servant-employment was very high and whose middle-class status is uncontested.[28] In 1856, at least 11 per cent of the Parisian doctors and 38 per cent of the lawyers did not employ a servant (without allowing for those who employed more than one).[29] In the Paris of 1872, fewer than three-quarters of the lawyers and pharmacists could have employed a single servant.[30] Only Parisian magistrates could have met the standard of servant-employment to qualify as middle-class among all of the liberal professions.[31] Thus, a sizeable proportion of the middle classes in the nineteenth century did not employ servants, most often in the early stages of marriage when resources were meagre but household demands were considerable.

Although it is important to realise that significant elements of the middle class were servant-less, the key point remains the new link between the middle classes and servants. Nineteenth-century domestic service received its peculiar character in part from the attitudes toward life which separated the middle classes from social groups above and below them. The nature of the master-servant relationship in the nineteenth century was at least partially a result of the attitudes of this new employer group.

During the nineteenth century traditional aspects of the master-servant relationship persisted but they were accompanied by the emergence of some new elements. Continuity was evident in the paternal role which many masters and mistresses assumed toward their servants. This paternal role was institutionalised by the legal inferiority of the domestic. Elaborate rules of etiquette which regulated the interaction between masters and mistresses and their servants also persisted into the nineteenth century which insisted upon the forms of deference.

The new elements which emerged in the course of the century showed the influence of the middle-class work and family ethic. Middle-class literature discussed the specific 'calling' of the woman to the role of wife and mother which reflected upon her ability to manage a household and to direct her servants. There were various indications of the attempts to rationalise domestic life in the same way that rational principles were being introduced into commercial and professional life. Ultimately, in response to this introduction of rationalisation into the master-servant relationship, the servants began to attempt to assimilate themselves into the working classes.

Following from the odd combination of certain traditional patterns and the introduction of some new attitudes, there was a third strand in masters' outlooks toward their servants that can best be characterised as an inability to see servants as individual human beings. The complaints in middle-class literature and especially in the household manuals suggested a general dissatisfaction of the employers with their servants. The dishonesty, laziness, and sexual promiscuity of servants were often exaggerated, but the attitude of employers which this literature reflected was in itself important to their relationship with their servants. At an extreme, this attitude seems to fit one well-known explanation of the outlook of the middle classes toward the urban lower classes —

including the servant group – the Louis Chevalier thesis on the middle-class phobia toward the 'dangerous classes.'[32]

Chevalier argued that the tone for the middle-class attitude toward the lower classes in the nineteenth century was set by the 'criminal theme' which can be found in middle-class literature. Balzac's work, for example, treated the problem of crime 'less by a description of the criminal milieu strictly speaking than by an evocation of this criminal potential which exudes from the masses and the popular quarters.'[33] Chevalier depicted the spectre of 'anonymous criminality' as the dominant element in the relationship of the middle classes to the urban popular classes – a criminality which was novel and even more frightening because it was faceless and ubiquitous. The demographic and economic transformation of Paris during the Restoration was the cause, Chevalier argued, of a general middle-class fear of the urban masses as dirty, unhealthy and definitely dangerous. The result was that the lower classes 'who were anxious to make a place for themselves in a hostile milieu', surrounded by the middle classes, were induced to 'abandon themselves to all hatreds, all violence, and all crimes.'[34]

Chevalier deals with servants in regard to the sexual exploitation by their employers which united servants with other segments of the working poor. Servants' lodgings also contributed to the overcrowded conditions of London and Paris which, as Chevalier notes, aroused middle-class disgust. Moreover, employers of servants at times justifiably complained about thefts by domestics. Finally, the work of Parent-Duchâtelet on Paris and that of Mayhew and Booth on London established the indisputable connection between domestic service and prostitution for many young women.[35]

When unemployed, servants seemed to merge into the urban masses and become part of the criminal milieu. In 1816, the prefect of police in Paris wrote in support of the imperial decree which made unemployed domestics subject to arrest as 'vagabonds'[36] and called them 'this turbulent class of society.'[37] In France this attitude had its foundation in the revolutionary era in which some domestics played a role. 'The excesses against their benefactors to which a great number of servants were carried has inspired a just hostility; one counts only on their ingratitude.'[38] But in England such an attitude was rarely expressed. The nuisance of domestic thefts and the occasional retelling of cases of servants' violence against employers were not generalised into the fear of one's servants. By contrast, this was the official French rationalisation for the system of work permits (*livrets*) for servants and for later schemes for placement agencies.

But even for France it would be misleading to adopt the Chevalier approach for the actual situation of servants.[39] Some of the reasons for this are obvious: most servants were female and not as inclined to violence as the male poor; servants were usually isolated from the influences of other popular elements, and once employed, servants were in constant, intimate contact with their employers. Servants were simply not viewed as an unknown, faceless mob who could inspire fear. Except for their association with other servants, which was limited, the majority of servants worked alone or with only one other domestic. Their only society consisted of whatever rapport could be established with the families which they served. Their relationship to the employer class was consequently nearly always on an individual basis. Therefore, the thesis of a middle-class fear of the urban masses does not explain the employer attitude toward servants, an important element of the lower classes, and the actual master-servant relationship has broader implications for the Chevalier thesis.

The argument was sometimes made that the employment of a servant offered the middle-class employer a unique opportunity for contact with the lower classes.[40] This opportunity would be a 'means to exercise generosity'[41] and to participate in the 'holy work' of moralising the lower classes.[42] Hence, one of the best-known of the French domestic economy manuals' authors, Madame Alq, argued that 'it is very good to propagate education in the poor classes' in order to encourage mistresses to teach their servants to read and to guide them in the selection of appropriate reading matter.[43] Similarly in England, Mrs Beeton emphasised that the training and supervision of servants was the most important responsibility of the mistress.[44] The contact between servant and mistress could be used as the means to communicate to the lower classes the habit of economy[45] — a habit well learned by servants. These arguments were a reflection of a paternal attitude toward the lower classes which found an important outlet in the relationship of the master to his servant. The motives involved did not characterise the actual behaviour of all employers in regard to their servants, but there is sufficient evidence of a greater benevolence toward an important element of the lower classes than the Chevalier thesis allows.

Paternalism was the dominant aspect of the master-servant relationship in the nineteenth century. It was the legacy of a much older life-style but it persisted in the nineteenth century and was often found mixed with more modern ideas of employer-employee relationships. Employers were urged to take more of a personal interest in their servants[46] and were warned that if all the good servants had disappeared it was because good mistresses were also lacking.[47] Even in the context of the International Feminist Congress in Paris in 1900, the paternalistic view of servants was expressed. A delegate, who objected to the suggestion that one day off a week be required for servants, argued that 'these children would not know what to do with an entire day off.'[48] And the feminist champion of servants' rights, Madame Vincent, accepted the attitude that servants needed to be 'protected' rather than 'organised.'[49]

The paternal role, however benevolent, provided the employer with extensive authority over the servant for his or her own good. This authority could sometimes be suffocating to the domestic, but it was justified as necessary to the important responsibility which the employer bore to train his servants. 'The domestic is, like the child, essentially an imitator, and rarely would one find a virtuous domestic in the home of a mean master.'[50]

The employer's responsibility was both legal and moral. In the legal sense the employer was liable for damage caused by his servant in the performance of his duties in the same way that an individual is liable if his dog bites another person.[51] The employer's moral responsibility was even more extensive since he or she represented the example of good conduct after whom the servant should pattern himself or herself.[52]

The employer's authority was not intended to be harsh. The manuals emphasised that the best means of assuring the servant's respect and deference was to be similarly polite when giving orders to the servants.[53] The ideal solution was to establish a rapport with one's servant as close as possible to the true parental one by taking a servant into one's home while still a child. The dependent relationship which defined a servant could then be established more easily and the servant could more easily be trained.[54] The master or mistress should earn the 'sacred title' by superior wisdom and magnanimity.[55]

This authoritarian paternalism left little room for the servant's freedom of action, but this was precisely the object. The employer's supposition was that servants would use their free time badly. As a turn-of-the-century English servant complained: 'I am hardly ever allowed out and special permission has to be obtained if I wish to post a letter.'[56] No 'respectable' mistress would allow her servant the opportunity to transgress moral laws,[57] as one mistress bluntly advised her newly hired servant: 'In this house one never goes out. . . This is a rule of the house . . . I will not pay servants in order that under the guise of seeing girl friends they go out to seek lovers.'[58] Servants often complained that in lieu of more leisure time, employers organised activities for them which were considered useful and healthy.[59] Madame Pariset in 1821 outlined an elaborate scheme for insuring servants' orderly and profitable conduct. The mistress was to spend evenings surveying and encouraging her servants to read books chosen by her and to copy them in order to perfect their handwriting. Such surveillance would be a benefit to the servants while eliminating the 'intolerable noise in the corridors which servants ordinarily make' when they are not busy.[60] The paternalism of the employers, while somewhat distasteful to servants, may have had significant unexpected benefits for the domestic who was thereby able to acquire a limited education.

The paternalism of servant-employers was diluted in the nineteenth century by the persistence of another traditional attitude – the expectation of deference. While traditional etiquette militated against contacts between masters and servants and set up a clear superior to inferior relationship, paternalism required the constant intervention of the employer on his servant's behalf. Although the effect of the rules of etiquette on actual conduct is very difficult to assess, the dilemma which it might raise was accurately described by Madame Pariset. 'In your frequent contacts, treat her with maternal benevolence, but do not suffer the indiscreet familiarity that this could produce.'[61] Deference to the employer was supposed to be paid by the servant's posture. The servant was expected to stand whenever the employer entered the room,[62] and a domestic did not walk beside her mistress in the street nor sit beside her in a carriage.[63] The rules of etiquette reinforced the 'bulkheads'[64] which separated the master from his servant and provided the middle-class mistress with the security of her superior social position.[65] 'In elaborated upper-class households,' a sociologist has argued, 'upper servants were crucial agents in the performance of deference ceremonies.'[66] The structures of etiquette were also clearly an attempt to exercise control over the behaviour of servants and this was both recognised and resented by some domestics.[67]

The servant's proper place in the social order was externalised by the uniform he or she wore, and mistresses seem to have been excessively concerned about servants' dress. The manuals commented endlessly on the appropriate clothing for domestic servants, and complained of the 'arrogance' of servants whose dress during their leisure hours imitated that of their employers.[68] This inclination of servants to shed their uniforms and dress like their employers was condemned as leading to deceit and insubordination.[69] Like the insistence upon servants' deferent behaviour, this concern with domestics' appearance underlines the impression that employers used servants to emphasise their own social position.

The social rules of deference were securely founded in the legal inferiority of the servant. The servant's employer had extensively rights to protect himself against his servant. The employer was at liberty to search his servant's room in order to assure himself of his servant's honesty.[70] Although this practice was denigrated as 'useless and degrading',[71] mention of it was not uncommon. Article 1781 of the French civil code stated that the master was to be believed on his affirmation in matters of the payment of wages. The stipulation provided the employer with a definitely superior standing in the eyes of the law — a great advantage in any legal dispute with a servant. This article, although attacked by the Luxembourg Commission of 1848, remained in force until 1868.[72]

Other elements in the master's legal superiority were even slower to change. A French legal commentary in 1925 noted that crimes committed by servants had always been more severely punished than similar types of crimes by others.[73] Stringent penalties attached to the chief domestic crimes such as theft or 'abuse of confidence' by a servant.[74] Yet the only recourse of an English servant who had been the victim of 'harsh, cruel, or immoral treatment' was to leave his or her employer and sue for one month's wages.[75] In spite of the responsibility of the employer to protect the young servants in his household, the customary punishment for his misuse of those servants was their removal from his service.[76]

The impact of the legal superiority of the employer should not be underestimated. Although few disputes between masters and servants were settled in courts of law, the moral force of the employer's superior legal position must have deterred the servant from seeking damages in a dispute. In both France and England, the servant was entitled to advance notice of dismissal (eight days' notice in France; as much as a month in England), but the master could dismiss a servant for any 'grave' motive without paying him.[77] The employer could also refuse to give the departing servant a 'character' or letter of reference without which it was very difficult to secure another position.[78] Moreover, in England the servant who left a position without just cause and without notice was liable to legal punishment.[79] The advantages of this kind of service contract were obviously one-sided.

Yet the traditions of paternalism and deference did not continue unabated. Signs of conflict appear in one traditional use of servants, which came under new attack as the middle class defined its own ethic. The tradition was the practice of employing servants to care for children, particularly the use of wet nurses. Here, distaste for infant care combined with reliance on a deferential lower class to produce a common pre-industrial pattern of behavior. One eighteenth-century source insisted that out of every 30 infants born in Paris in that century, 29 had been nursed by wet nurses.[80] The figure is undoubtedly highly exaggerated, but even so, there is no question that the practice was common; and more significant is the fact that it began to decline rapidly by the nineteenth century. The use of wet nurses remained much more widespread in France than in England in the nineteenth century; in 1886, 28.3 per cent of the children born in Paris were still put out to wet nurses.[81] The practice had declined significantly in England by this time,[82] although the 'baby farms' or wet nurses who accepted more charges than they could reasonably handle, probably continued to operate for the working classes or mothers with illegitimate children. And the use of wet nurses by English mothers was still widespread enough to disturb English doctors.[83]

The practice of using wet nurses threatened middle-class family life with a variety of dangers. The servant in whose care children were to be confided had to be selected carefully in regard to her health and morals. Some French doctors became very concerned in the nineteenth century about the incidence of tuberculosis among domestics[84] and about the possibility of contamination of infants by syphilitic nurses.[85]

Moreover, a servant could come between the parent and the child, for 'a mother who could not share with the domestic the care which the first years of the infant's life requires could expect a preference of the infant for his servant.'[86] This signalled a conflict of interest for middle-class parents in both France and England who viewed servants as a mark of their social status but who wished to maintain or develop a very close relationship with their children.[87] It also reflected some difficulty in continuing to regard servants as traditional inferiors. This ambivalence bore heavily on the attitude of mistresses or masters toward servants who were parent-surrogates, and especially the wet nurses. How much this attitude may have affected the master-servant relationship is almost impossible to judge, although this theme seems to have underlaid much of the criticism of the character of wet nurses. And this in turn means that the purely traditional paternal relationship by which the servant was expected to perform customary tasks dutifully had begun to erode.

New elements in the master-servant relationship became obvious as the middle classes began to set the tone for early industrial culture by their emphasis on self-discipline and the importance of work. The transformation was by no means confined to the middle classes; the middle-class work and family ethic gradually permeated most levels of society. Work set the framework for daily life and family life in turn provided the goals for work. This double focus of the middle-class ethic underlined the significance of domestic tranquillity – the wife's responsibility – and required a great many talents from the housewife to produce domestic efficiency.

The burden of domestic work has always fallen heavily on the shoulders of the wife, but the middle-class wife of the nineteenth century felt the burden more deeply because of two novel aspects of her situation: the newness of her role as mistress of servants and the emphasis of the middle classes on the particular 'calling' of the middle-class woman. Except for the wives of small merchants who were true partners in the work of their husband's shop, the middle-class wife was generally confined to the work of the house.[88] The life of the family provided her important but limited role in the world since she did not participate in professional or civic life to any great extent.

Much was made of the idea that household work was the woman's 'profession'. In fact, the manuals themselves were an important result of the attempted 'professionalisation' of housework. Like her husband's occupation in running a shop or managing a factory, a middle-class housewife's job was to maintain and direct a well-run house. The wife had the tacit authority (if not the full legal sanction) to hire and fire servants.[89] Sarah Stickney Ellis argued in 1843 that 'the perfection of good domestic management required so many excellencies both of head and heart, as to render it a study well worth the attention of the most benevolent and enlightened of human beings.'[90] The achievement in the nineteenth century of the title of mistress of the household was a significant one for women because it represented a clear concession of a sphere of power which was specifically female. And if men denigrated household work as unimportant, argued Harriet Prescott Spofford in 1881, it was probably because men were jealous of this important authority which women exercised in the home.[91]

One of the problems of the housewife at the beginning of the nineteenth century was her lack of training for her 'profession'. The middle- and upper-class women received little education and rarely any training in household affairs. Consequently, her newness to the position of mistress may sometimes have hindered her in the running of an increasingly complex household. This complaint was voiced constantly throughout the century both in the domestic economy manuals and in the comments of reformers.

> It is only too true that the best schools, where the young people receive the best education, lack completely this primary element, this fundamental principle of true education; that which makes a good housewife and, consequently, a worthy spouse and a respectable mother.[92]

The role that the housewife had to play required at least as much knowledge of domestic skills as would be necessary if she had to perform all of the household chores herself. The mistress-servant relationship in the nineteenth century thus involved the socialisation of both. The mistress learned to give orders and supervise work,[93] while teaching the servant to do a respectable job.[94] The servant was trained by the submission to a new work discipline and by the contact with middle-class values.

Only in the 1880s, when the scarcity of servants was becoming increasingly obvious, were schools for teaching home economics used for teaching young women the techniques of running a house and caring for children without the assistance of a servant.[95] A report on such training in the department of the Nord in 1909 indicated clear recognition that this problem was still unsolved. The report advised the teaching of household economy to middle-class girls because 'her task, in fact, is *complicated* by the fact that she has under her orders one or more servants.'[96] Until the end of the nineteenth century, however, domestic economy education for most women was a notable failure both in France and in England.[97] Even among young women whose modest position precluded the employment of a servant, there was a lack of interest in domestic work and of experience in running a household.[98] The repeated treatment of the same problems in household economy manuals throughout the century suggest that the manuals were not sufficient in themselves to solve them.

The middle-class application of the principle of rationalisation to domestic life, even if not invariably effective, also had an important impact on domestic service. The household economy manuals are filled with examples of the permeation of daily life by the strictures of time schedules and account keeping. Keeping household accounts of monetary transactions were not uncommon. What is remarkable is the even broader concern for orderliness and accountability; mistresses, for example, were urged to keep careful inventories of provisions, of linens, of china.[99] This almost obsessive concern with possessions was often regarded as part of middle-class character by contemporary observers,[100] but seen in wider scope, it was part of a general concern with efficiency in housekeeping.

The domestic economy manuals themselves offer ample proof of this characteristic of nineteenth-century housekeeping — the concern for orderliness and efficiency. The housewife's day was carefully detailed from the first moment to the last, stretching from early morning through the final tasks of her day. Mrs Beeton's description of part of that schedule was very typical. The middle-class housewife was expected to depend very heavily upon domestic help to perform the labour of household duties, but she had to superintend that work and in particular to pay attention to the care received by the children.[101] Before breakfast, she had to see that the children were properly washed and dressed, then came breakfast, and after it, rounds of the kitchen and other rooms to check that the morning's work was being performed by the servants. 'The orders for the day should then be given; and any questions which the domestics desire to ask, respecting their several departments, should be answered, and any special articles they may require handed to them from the store-closet.'[102] Much of the rest of the morning and afternoon could be spent in reading or making social calls, according to Beeton. However, this vision of a housewife's time schedule was realistic only for those households served by several domestics and did not fit the situation of the woman whose only domestic assistance was a single maid-of-all-work. For the latter, the time schedules set out by the manuals were more elaborate and understandably much more demanding. In all, as much as a third of the text of typical domestic economy manuals dealt with the use of time. Since recipes and instructions for performing domestic tasks took up at least half of the pages of most manuals, this concern with time schedules is striking and characteristic.[103]

The use of time was an important aspect of housekeeping efficiency and it was related to the introduction of a new kind of work discipline with industrialisation, typified by factory work but touching many aspects of life. The manuals counselled mistresses upon how to make the greatest profit from the expenditure of her own energies and those of her servants, attempting to train her and her servants to think about household work in a very novel way. It was this aspect of nineteenth-century housekeeping which servants often resented, but Lavinia

Swainbank, who became a housemaid in the 1890s, recalled this rigorous training without rancour when she wrote in her autobiography:

> Here I was to familiarise myself with the Timetable. I had never before seen one of these and on first sight I could not see how one could possibly perform these duties in one day. This proved a splendid basic training, turning an ordinary human being into something resembling a well-oiled machine whose rhythm and motion ran smoothly like a clock. To this day I have not lost the clockwork precision instilled into me by a succession of head housemaids and timetables forty-eight years ago.[104]

The stress on efficiency could mean an increased pace of work and more careful supervision to induce work discipline without allowing the servant the opportunity of leaving work after the day was done.[105] Like the time and work discipline of the factory, this emphasis on efficiency was part of industrialisation but its application was a slow and not always linear evolution.

Despite such indications of an attempt to rationalise domestic life, the ample supply of servants slowed the full rationalisation of housework. In order to economise, the middle-class mistress might select a maid who could perform many tasks including that of a laundress in order to avoid sending the laundry out,[106] a move which ran counter to the specialisation of labor. Since most households had only one or, at best, two servants, the kinds of tasks which a domestic performed were rarely very specialised. Since the trend in the nineteenth century was toward a decline in the number of servants employed, this countered the rationalisation of domestic economy as fewer servants were sought to perform an increasingly wider range of jobs.[107] As long as domestic labour was cheap during the transitional stages of industrialisation, the stimulus for technological improvements was lacking. The continued insistence of the domestic economy manuals suggests that few households met the rigid standards of efficiency which the manuals described.

Extension of the work relationship into domestic life meant that both employer and servant began to think in terms of a commercial exchange of services for money. The 'labour as commodity' idea was advanced by articulate servants who saw it as a solution to some of the problems of mistreatment and degradation. If their labour were treated as valuable, one English servant argued, domestics could not be considered as totally inferior beings by their employers.[108] A French lawyer noted the change in domestic service by 1896 but insisted that the employer class was at fault. 'The masters today believe to have done everything necessary for their servants when they have regularly paid their wages. It is their principal error . . . to no longer consider servants as anything but mercenary workers . . .'[109] Both English and French employers were ambivalent in their attitudes toward this change. While some argued that domestic service needed to change since it was 'out of harmony with modern ideals',[110] others deplored the situation which put master-servant relationships on a cash basis.[111]

Consequently, the nature of the master-servant relationship in the nineteenth century was a mixture of several elements. Some aspects of the traditional relationship persisted, notably the paternal role of the master reinforced both by legal liability and by a feeling of moral responsibility for the servant. There were also important new elements in the relationship which reflected the influence of the middle-class employment of servants. Some further indication of the significance of these new elements to actual employer behaviour can be drawn from French sources on two kinds of gifts made to servants.

In Flaubert's *Madame Bovary*, on the occasion of an agricultural fair, a servant received a silver medal and 25 francs for her fifty-four years of service with the same master.[112] This practice of awarding prizes for long service with the same family is typical of the middle-class penchant for awarding acts of individual achievement, though there seems to have been no English equivalent of these awards. The first prizes were awarded by the Society of the Sciences and of Morals in Versailles in 1838, and each year several prizes were awarded to servants such as the recipient in 1868, Jeanne-Antoine Bourgeois. Mademoiselle Bourgeois had served forty-eight years in the same family of a cultivator, caring for her mistress during an eighteen-month illness which required constant care and afterward during the last ten years of her mistress's life, unwilling to retire until after the old woman's death.[113] Prizes were also awarded each year from 1847 by the Académie française, for which the Académie always received an ample number of nominations.[114] Most of the recipients had served the same family for over thirty years, and in addition, had 'sacrificed everything in order not to abandon masters who had fallen into indigence . . .'[115] The prizes and the acts of loyalty which they honoured do not suggest any trace of the Chevalier description of middle-class fear of the lower classes. They do reflect middle-class belief in and encouragement of the individuals who fulfilled their expected roles in serving the middle and upper classes. Probably the prizes also indicate middle-class concern over what they considered to be a decline in lower-class deference and increasing class tensions.

Another index of master-servant relationships were the gifts given to loyal servants at their masters' deaths. Again the evidence is sketchy and provides only a few examples of what may be assumed to be exceptional cases. A sampling of the wills of individuals who died in Paris in 1853 yields seven examples of gifts to servants.[116] One man whose fortune totalled 53,000 francs left over 12,000 francs to his unmarried female domestic, and another man bequeathed over 6,000 francs to his cook. The other five individuals, with fortunes ranging from 17,000 francs to over 274,000 francs, provided their servants with an annual income for life of between 200 and 400 francs. Even the smallest gift was generous, approximating the servant's annual wages. Most of the gifts were made to specific servants who had merited their masters' gratitude, but one woman left 300 francs to any servant who had been in her service for at least two years.[117] The examples suggest again the middle-class encouragement of individuals capable of great loyalty and diligence in the performance of their jobs. The practice of death bequests also was closely tied to the paternalistic tradition in which the employer was expected to take care of the servant when he or she had grown too old to remain in active service and death bequests fulfilled this responsibility.

It is probable that there were similar bequests made to servants by English employers, especially among the upper classes who employed large household staffs. But the paternalistic tradition was weaker in England than in France. The English middle classes by the middle of the nineteenth century were much closer than the French to accepting a contractual relationship between masters and servants like that of employers and employees. English mistresses had been introduced through women's magazines and the increasing activity of women's organisations to the idea that servants should be treated like other workers. On the other side of the Channel, the women's movement was almost insignificant by the turn of the twentieth century and even the vanguard of French feminists continued either to ignore the problems of domestic servants or to encourage a more traditional mistress-servant relationship. But in England, women's organisations such as the Central Bureau for the Employment of Women were active in arguing for change in the status of domestic service because it was 'an occupation in which modern conditions of labour are unrecognised, or at any rate an occupation out of harmony with modern ideals.'[118]

The amalgam of the persistence of certain traditional attitudes and the introduction of rationalising elements produces a strange mixture, yet there is evidence that all of these elements were present to some degree in the master-servant relationship in the nineteenth century. However benevolent or paternal some employers were, the servant was not considered by them to be a human being with rights and abilities, according to the conclusions of a study by the Women's Industrial Council of Great Britain in 1916. As Christina Butler reported for the Council, 'a common complaint is not to be treated as a human being.'[119] Much earlier, Madame Alq, after describing her plans for the education and moral guidance of her servants, concluded with this self-defeating rationale: '. . . it is necessary to take the pain to moralise them; to condescend to concern yourself with them a little, and hope that servants are beings which resemble us in having a mind and a heart.'[120]

Yet there remains considerable evidence of the reality of paternalism in the master-servant relationship. The death bequests are one of the indications of the survival of paternalism. The number of exceptional servants who were honoured by prizes also suggests that the devoted, familial connections between some masters and servants were as true in 1910 as they had been a century before. Juliette Sauget's memoirs provide an additional personal testimony to the paternalism which continued to characterise master-servant relationships in the decade before the First World War: Juliette's mistress wanted to send her to a cooking school so that she could qualify for a better job.[121] But the existence of paternalism does not rule out the exploitation of a servant by an employer for which paternalism provided the theoretical justification, and this is a question which will be taken up elsewhere.

Gradually the influence of the middle classes was paring away the remnants of paternalism, rationalising domestic life and transforming the master-servant relationship into an employer-employee relationship. The middle-class attitude in the nineteenth century toward its servants was less characterised by fear or disdain than by their need to assert their social superiority over their servants, the economy — sometimes the avariciousness — with which the middle classes utilised time and money, and their stress on the role of the middle-class woman whose world was shaped by the household and her family.

Obviously, the middle-class sources, upon which this analysis of attitudes has been largely based, tend to reflect the more generous, the more high-minded and altruistic aspects of employer attitudes because the manuals were meant to be uplifting for their readers. Hence the real impact of these attitudes upon the conditions of the servant class are somewhat obscured. Beyond the limited examples of the application of these attitudes which are discussed in this chapter, the middle-class outlook needs further testing against the actual conduct of most masters and mistresses. Consequently, the general policy of masters toward servants will be analysed in later chapters on the appalling living and working conditions of servants, prevalent hiring and firing practices, and the symptoms of alienation and disaffection among servants.

Yet the problems which plagued the master-servant relationship in the nineteenth century were not due only to the failure of one social class to understand another and to the influence of the new employer class's own attitudes, but also to the nature of the individuals who entered domestic service during the nineteenth century. The evolution of domestic service must thus be studied in terms of the change in the individuals who became domestics, even as the evolving, often confusing, attitudes of the employer class inevitably coloured the lives of the new servants.

2. URBAN MIGRATION

The history of domestic service in the nineteenth century is the story of urban migration. Millions of young women and men translated their need for work into a move to the growing cities. Pushed off the overburdened land by declining agricultural fortunes and increasing insecurity of tenures, these individuals faced considerable problems in seeking urban employment – in England primarily because of the overabundant supply of unskilled labour; in France because of the character of industrial development. Domestic service helped to bridge the gap between population growth and the widening of occupational opportunities. Service thus acted as a holding category for the surplus rural population until occupational opportunities, particularly for women, broadened sufficiently to absorb the increase in urban population.

The study of domestic servants' migration is an analysis not only of where servants moved but also why they moved. It is crucial to know why individuals entered domestic service in the nineteenth century, for this factor is linked to their perception of the occupation and to their own expectations upon entering that occupation. Domestic service in the nineteenth century was changing – becoming more highly urbanised, feminised, and commercialised – and it is important to know whether or not the motivations of the individuals entering servanthood were also changing. Domestic service was no longer simply a traditional occupation for rural-born individuals; it was also an active modernising agent which facilitated urban acculturation and occupational mobility in the urban environment. Thus, the reasons why individuals entered servanthood may indicate why domestic service was preferred over other kinds of employment and why servants were better prepared for integration into the urban environment than many other lower-class individuals, urban as well as rural.

Domestic service reached its peak during the early decades of industrialisation. Between 1830 and 1885, approximately 15 per cent of all French households employed one or more servants.[1] In the same period, one in every six English women was a domestic; and one of every five single women was listed as a servant.[2] The servant class grew rapidly in the nineteenth century until about 1880 and then began to decline (Tables 2.1 and 2.2). The Parisian segment of the servant class, however, continued to grow after the overall decline of servants was established, so that after 1880 there was an ever-higher concentration of servants in the capital city (Fig. 2.3). In contrast, the servant population in London followed the national trend, gradually levelling

off about 1890 and very slowly declining in percentage terms
(Table 2.4). Thus, the growth of the urban servant class paralleled the
peak period of urbanisation and declined when that peak had passed.[3]

Urban domestic servants in the nineteenth century were generally of
agricultural backgrounds, for the cities failed to provide a sufficient
supply of servants.[4] During the middle of the century, the demand of
the growing middle class for domestic help could only be satisfied by an
almost ceaseless flow of immigrants from the countryside. Among the
servants in Versailles in 1820, 61 per cent had been born outside of the
department, while 24 per cent had been born in the department but
outside of Versailles. Less than 15 per cent of the servants working in
Versailles in 1820 had been born there.[5] In 1872, only 4 per cent of
the male servants and 6 per cent of the female who were working in
Versailles had been born there.[6] This pattern is similar to that
discovered by Adeline Daumard's study of Paris in 1831 which traced
servant origins from their death records. Here, 60 per cent of the
servants who died in Paris had been born outside the city.[7] London
between 1851 and 1871 also drew 60 per cent of its servants from
outside the city.[8] In fact, servants demonstrated consistently higher
average geographical mobility than any other job category: in France
in 1901, 48 per cent of the servants were working outside their natal
departments while only 30 per cent of the industrial workers were.[9] By
the end of the nineteenth century, industrial occupations were
displaying a much higher concentration of origins than ever before
while servants continued to travel longer distances to seek work.[10]

Table 2.1. French servant population

	Servants	% of Total Population	% of Active Population
1851	906,666	2.5	
1861	896,952	2.4	
1866	900,964	2.4	14.6
1872	949,269	2.6	14.0
1876	1,014,249	2.8	
1881	1,156,604	3.1	
1886	1,078,961	2.8	
1891	925,892	2.4	
1896	916,970	2.4	4.5
1901	956,195	2.5	
1906	946,293	2.4	
1911	929,548	2.4	4.6
1921	787,385	2.0	

Source: *Annuaire statistique de la France*, LXVI, 32-4; *Statistique
générale de la France*, 1851-1921.

Table 2.2. English servant population

	Servants	% of Labour Force
1831	665,709	12.6
1841	1,165,233*	14.5
1851	908,138	13.0
1861	1,123,428	14.3
1871	1,387,872	15.3
1881	1,453,175	15.4
1891	1,549,502	15.8
1901	1,370,773	14.1
1911	1,314,024	13.9

Source: *Census of England and Wales,* 1831 through 1911; Deane and
Cole, *British Industrial Growth, 1688-1959,* p.142.

*The 1841 census categories for indoor domestic servants are not
comparable to successive censuses.

Table 2.3. Servant population in Paris

	Total Number of Servants	Percentage of Parisian Population	Percentage of Servant Class
1846	67,554	7.7	7.5
1861	111,496	6.1	12.4
1872	112,031	6.1	11.8
1891	185,756	7.7	20.1
1901	207,201	7.8	21.7
1911	194,346	6.7	20.9
1921	191,335	6.6	24.3

Source: *Statistique générale de la France.*

Table 2.4. Servant population in London

	Total Number of Servants	Percentage of Servant Class
1851	195,490	21.5
1861	226,816	20.2
1871	262,083	18.9
1881	255,440	17.6
1891	255,440	16.5
1911	214,270	16.3
1921	181,980	14.8

Source: *Census of England and Wales.*

Not surprisingly there are some indications that in more highly urbanised England, more servants were drawn from the urban populations. Rural depopulation had proceeded more rapidly in England so that the traditional source of domestic labour was disappearing.[11] Rowntree insisted that two-thirds of the servant girls in York had come from that city,[12] though York was unusual in offering almost no alternative industrial employment. Thus, outside of London whose immigrant servant population was as large as that of Paris, English servants may have been more heavily drawn from urban districts after the mid-nineteenth century.[13] The evidence is, however, highly impressionistic, and the image of the English servant remains the naive and rather crude country girl.[14] And in spite of the fact that one-quarter of London's servants had been born in that city, the urban-born in England were less likely to become servants than the rural-born.

Despite the unusual geographical mobility involved in urban servanthood, domestic service was a very traditional occupation for young peasants. In the eighteenth century the 'servante' formed up to 13 per cent of the urban population of France, mostly drawn from the immediately surrounding countryside and employed in a combination of household and industrial tasks.[15] The system of poor relief in England had been a customary source of domestic labour since single women were only entitled to relief if they accepted employment.[16] Even more important was the Old Régime custom of a kind of domestic 'apprenticeship', in which the sons and daughters of tenant farmers served in neighbouring farm households and constituted members of the extended household.[17] Thus, young peasants who entered domestic service in the nineteenth century were following a traditional pattern in which temporary service at a neighbouring farm allowed the individual to help support his or her parents[18] or to accumulate a small dowry before marriage at an age of 25 or later.[19] A certain proportion of these young peasants had always exercised the option of migrating to one of the large cities and exchanging one kind of domestic position for another, though most eighteenth-century servants had remained close to their natal villages.[20] The unprecedented geographical mobility of most nineteenth-century servants did not mean the end of the traditional rural pattern. As late as 1900 this rural pattern was described in the rare memoir of a French servant, Juliette Sauget:

> . . . as soon as the school years were ended we had to be placed in neighbouring farms in individual households in order to help our very poor parents. In this way, all my brothers and sisters had been field-workers and household servants [both called domestics] for a certain period of time.[21]

The persistence of the pre-industrial pattern of temporary domestic service meant that traditional socialisation undoubtedly played a major role in guiding individuals into domestic service. Yet the nineteenth century introduced some vital differences in this pattern, within the context of very high geographical mobility. The too-numerous sons and daughters of a landless peasantry could not expect their period in service to be interrupted by a call to work the family land. Thus the increased urbanisation of domestic service and the decline of agricultural employment established the channel for the permanent urban migration of many domestics. Out of Juliette Sauget's family of five brothers and four sisters, at least two of the girls chose to seek better domestic positions in Paris and settled there. Many other young men and women of this class followed the same path in the nineteenth century.

Any explanation of the persistent importance of domestic service must be sufficiently complex to allow for both the 'push' and 'pull' factors in this kind of occupational migration. In other words, the movement of many young peasants into urban domestic service was not simply dictated by necessity, but was often the result of the attraction which the cities and household service itself exercised on young men and women. Analysis of the geographic origins of French servants reveals the significance of both 'push' and 'pull' factors, for there was a movement away from the poorer agricultural departments, but also a substantial amount of long-range migration away from areas where industrial employment was available, as for example, in the Nord or the Bas-Rhin (see Figs. 2.1, 2.2, 2.3, 2.4). The patterns of servant migration thus deserve closer examination.

Much of servant migration was due to a kind of classic demographic response. A typical reaction of poor areas to the crisis of overpopulation is the siphoning off of excess children into domestic 'apprenticeships' outside the area.[22] Marginal peasant farmers in the French provinces with the highest birth rates sent so many of their daughters into service in Paris that the Breton servant-girl became almost synonymous with domestic service in Paris (Fig. 2.3).[23] Another obvious example of this phenomenon is the referral of English poor relief recipients to domestic positions, which we have already noted.

Agricultural decline and the impoverishment of segments of the peasantry forced young peasants to migrate at an earlier age. The overall age structure of the servant population, consequently, shows a large and increasing group under 24 among female servants (Table 2.5). English servants were younger on the whole than French servants; the largest group of English domestics fell between the ages of 15 and 24 rather than between 25 and 34 as in the French case (Table 2.6). English servant population was growing somewhat younger in the middle of the nineteenth century. This was as naked a 'push' factor as one could wish for. France, less pressed by agricultural/demographic stress, nonetheless saw countless people forced to leave the countryside, and servanthood provided a refuge. England, with its younger servant population, shows the results of such pressure even more keenly, where it struck both urban and rural elements.

One result of the new push factors – a vital change in the character of domestic service in the nineteenth century as servanthood became more highly urbanised – was the feminisation of service. Much of this process had already been accomplished by the period of the first published censuses; estimates of pre-revolutionary Paris suggest that male servants constituted one in every four males residing in some aristocratic sections.[24] The revolutionary period had depleted the ranks of male servants in both France and England and the nineteenth-century servant class never approached eighteenth-century levels of male employment in service. By the middle of the nineteenth century, the English servant class was already substantially feminised (Table 2.7). But both the French and English servant populations experienced a further decline in male employment in this sector as the nineteenth century drew to a close. This pattern of feminisation fits a characteristic model for industrialising societies.[25] In general, during the intermediate stage of economic development, the personal services sector is very large; urbanisation creates a demand for service personnel in bars and restaurants as well as in the homes of the newly-rich entrepreneurial class. Domestic labour becomes commercialised and absorbs a large segment of the unskilled labour which migrates to the urban centres. Gradually, however, the men move into the modernising sectors of the economy, leaving the females confined to the service sector by restrictive social values and by their lack of training. The women are slower to leave service for other employment, and consequently, the service sector is largely feminised at this stage.[26]

Male servants made the choice to seek other employment first. After 1880, the accelerating feminisation of domestic service in France can largely be explained on the basis of the defections of male servants because their economic position was being eroded by the levelling-off of servants' wages.[27] But in England there was almost a reversal of the trend toward feminisation between 1880 and 1900. This may mean that English wage trends were different or that English servants were less sensitive to these trends. But the pattern also suggests the proportionate increase of large household staffs, in which male servants were employed, as the number of single-servant households declined. In any case, female servants in both countries were much more reluctant to abandon service as an employment option throughout the nineteenth century.

The suggestion that individuals were leaving servanthood or were choosing alternative employment rather than enter the occupation brings us back to the question of 'push' and 'pull'. Although most migration was dictated by poverty or overpopulation or lack of occupational opportunities, the 'push' factor, the goal of that

Fig. 2.1. Geographic origins of servants in Lyons in 1872 (Percentages of Total Servants)

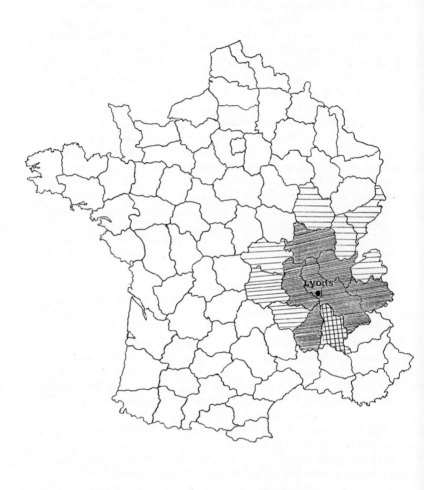

0 – 0.5%		2.0 – 3.9%	
0.6 – 1.9%		4.0% –	

Source: A. D. du Rhône, Série M, XI-XXIII (Lyon), Listes nominatives du dénombrement de la population de Lyon en 1872. Note: The 1872 census was the only manuscript census to list exact place of birth among the nineteenth-century censuses.

**Fig. 2.2. Geographic origins of servants in Versailles in 1872
(Percentages of Total Servants)**

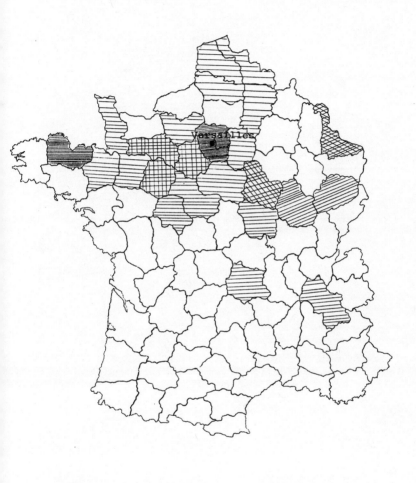

0 – 0.5%		2.0 – 3.9%
0.6 – 1.9%		4.0% –

Source: A. D. des Yvelines, 9 M 954^{12}, Listes nominatives du dénombrement
de la population de Versailles en 1872. Note: The 1872 and 1876 censuses of
Versailles were the only nineteenth-century manuscript census lists to include
exact place of birth.

**Fig. 2.3. Geographic origins of female servants in Paris in 1901
(Including the banlieue). (Percentages of Total Servants)**

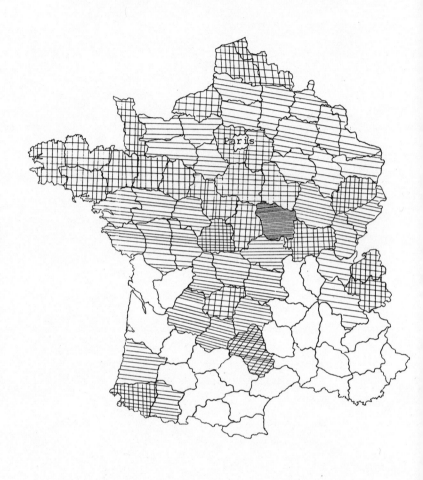

0 – 0.5%		2.0 – 3.9%	
0.6 – 1.9%		4.0% –	

Source: Statistique générale de la France, 1901, I, 328-9; 1901, IV, 428-9;
    1901, IV, 508-11. The manuscript censuses for the city of Paris before 1921
    no longer exist; hence, the published census for the year 1901 was used since
    it was the first published census to provide the information for this kind
    of analysis.

**Fig 2.4. Geographic origins of male servants in Paris in 1901
(Including the banlieue). (Percentages of Total Servants)**

0 — 0.5%   2.0 — 3.9%
0.6 — 1.9%   4.0% —

Source: Statistique générale de la France, 1901, I, 328-9; IV, 428-9; IV,
  508-11. The manuscript censuses for the city of Paris before 1921 no longer
  exist; hence, the published census for the year 1901 was used since this was
  the first published census to provide the information for this kind of analysis.

43

Table 2.5. Age structure of French servant population

	Versailles 1820 Males %	Versailles 1820 Females %	Versailles 1872 Males %	Versailles 1872 Females %	Lyons 1872 Males %	Lyons 1872 Females %
Under 14	1.3	0.5	0.7	0.8	1.6	0.5
15-19	10.2	9.9	9.8	11.0	15.2	10.9
20-24	14.0	20.5	17.3	21.4	14.5	35.1
25-34	30.0	25.3	28.8	30.2	36.4	28.7
35-44	16.7	16.1	24.9	16.6	20.0	13.0
45-54	10.9	12.7	12.2	11.5	9.1	7.6
55-64	11.2	9.0	4.4	5.6	1.9	3.1
65-	5.4	5.7	1.9	2.8	1.3	1.1

Source: Versailles, Listes nominatives, 1820, 1872; Lyon, Listes
  nominatives, 1872.

France 1901

	Servants Males %	Servants Females %	Total Active Population Males %	Total Active Population Females %	
Under 20	16.6	26.1	15.7	20.1	Under 21
20-24	6.8	14.7	9.2	10.2	21-24
25-29	15.0	12.4	11.2	10.7	
30-34	12.9	9.1	10.3	9.7	
35-39	11.4	7.8	10.0	9.3	
40-44	9.4	6.7	9.2	8.6	
45-49	7.6	5.8	8.2	7.7	
50-54	6.0	5.4	7.3	7.2	
55-64	9.1	8.0	11.6	10.6	
65-	5.2	4.0	7.3	5.9	

Source: *Statistique générale,* 1901, IV, 219 ff.; 1901, IV, 512.
  Foreigners are not included in these totals.

migration, was governed by tradition or choice. A striking example of
traditional patterns of migration in search of domestic employment
was the centuries-long tradition followed by residents of the French
Alpine regions. From the town of Passy in Haute-Savoie, the migrants
always went to Paris and never elsewhere, even though the rest of the
department sent its sons and daughters to Lyons, a much shorter
journey, to work as servants or unskilled labourers.[28] Migration might
thus be dictated by necessity, but where one migrated was not.

Because domestic service was a highly traditional occupation, the
patterns of domestic migration established precedents which facilitated

Table 2.6. Age structure of English servant population

	London, 1851		England and Wales, 1851	
	Male Indoor Servants	Female Indoor Servants	Female Servants	
	%	%		%
Under 15	5.2	5.7	Under 15	8.7
15-19	18.0	27.2	15-19	31.7
20-24	18.0	26.8	20-24	26.0
25-29	16.0	15.2	25-29	13.0
30-34	12.0	8.0	30-34	6.4
35-39	8.6	4.8	35-39	3.8
40-44	6.9	3.6	40-44	2.8
45-49	5.0	2.5	45-49	4.7
50-54	3.95	2.1	50-54	1.9
55-59	2.1	1.3	55-59	1.1
60-64	1.9	1.3	60-64	1.1
65-69	0.9	0.8	65-69	0.7
70-74	0.7	0.6	70-74	0.6
Over 75	0.4	0.6	Over 75	0.6

England and Wales
Female Servants

	1851	1861	1871	1881	1911
Under 15	8.7	8.9	11.6	8.0	3.1
15-19	31.7	38.1	30.2	35.0	28.3
20-24	26.0	23.6	23.6	24.5	25.4
25-44	26.0	26.3	19.7	24.0	32.3
45-64	8.8	8.8	5.3	7.2	9.5
65-	1.9	1.9	1.7	1.4	1.3

Source: *Census of England and Wales.*

Table 2.7. Male-female distribution of servants

	France		England	
	Males	Females	Males	Females
	%	%	%	%
1851	31.7	68.3	10.1	89.9
1861	30.9	69.1	8.5	91.5
1871	29.2	70.8	7.6	92.4
1881	29.8	70.2	8.9	91.1
1891	24.4	75.6	—	—
1901	18.0	82.0	8.5	91.5
1911	17.1	82.9	7.9	91.7

further migration. While searching for a domestic position, young immigrants could stay with relatives already residing in Paris or with other former natives of the same area, many of whom had originally established themselves in the city as servants. This informal network was almost certainly the most extensive channel for the placement of domestics in the city.[29] Within one apartment house or city block, it was common to find a great percentage of the servants from the same small area of the countryside. Once established, this channel encouraged further migration by facilitating the securing of a position and by making the move to the city easier. Moreover, reliance on relatives or other natives of the same area facilitated the transition to the urban environment and lessened the effect of the long-range migration.[30]

So there could be a persuasive argument that servanthood constituted the barest modification of traditional patterns for peasant youth, the minimum required by growing population pressure. The modification included some surprisingly long-range movement, but there is still more involved, as the cases of Paris and London — persistent centres of attraction for extensive geographical displacement — demonstrate. The continuing popularity of the capital cities reflected the higher salaries there as well as the pull of large urban centres. 'The larger the city, the greater its power of attraction,' according to Adna Weber's classic study of the nineteenth-century city.[31] But the cases of Paris and London are only the extremes of a more general pattern in domestic migration. Lyons or Birmingham would offer similar examples of substantial long-range migration. The longer distance covered by migrants who sought domestic positions in the cities suggests greater venturesomeness than the short-range migration of those who sought factory work. In following the traditional path of domestic service, then, servants may well have been attempting to assure themselves of a better future by hoping to profit from the clear advantages which domestic positions offered. In the context of the 'push' factor, there was the further fact that some people opted for urban service, while others, like some of Juliette Sauget's siblings, stayed closer to home. Why did some go and others not? Here we must invoke, if we cannot completely explain, personality differences and the possibility that certain individuals were open to the notion of novelty and venture to a greater extent than the norm. This was vital for women who, as servants, moved far from their families and into a world which, even if defined by tradition and cushioned by relatives, must have seemed strange in prospect.

The migration pattern of domestic servants and the constant supply of domestic labour suggest some important modifications of the conceptualisation of labour migration, precisely because of the distinctive combination of high geographical mobility, traditionalism, and the unique advantages of domestic service — which adds up, after all, to an assessment of human motives in a period of undeniable social upheaval. The classic theory of labour migration is Arthur Redford's statement that short-range migration characterised virtually all types of labour migration. 'The majority of the migrants to the towns came from the immediately surrounding counties, their places in turn being taken by migrants from places further away.'[32] This conventional theory has been applied directly to the migration of female workers: 'women are greater migrants than men, but move only short distances.'[33] Although the pattern of domestic migration does not refute Redford's thesis of short-range migration as the norm, it does indicate that many workers, and particularly females, migrated long distances without moving from job to job at intermediate towns along the way. The key point is that rural emigrants moved great distances in search of domestic employment even in some cases when industrial employment was available closer at hand, and this returns us to the question of the 'pull' of domestic service.

The failure of young women to seek industrial employment rather than continuing to enter servanthood may demonstrate nothing more than the inaccessibility of factory work or other industrial employment for women. The relatively low percentage of women who worked in French factories, compared to their English sisters, might reflect French employers' reluctance to employ women, forcing women to choose the more traditional option of domestic work — in other words, a simple push factor. But the rapid rise in women workers' wages as early as the July Monarchy in France implies the opposite[34] — that employers were in general more willing to employ women than French women were to work in factories. Here again, we must return to the question of motivation in speculating whether servants were choosing domestic service over other occupations because they recognised its attractive aspects.

There was clearly a prejudice against factory work for women in the nineteenth century. Women were supposed to make better wives if they became domestic servants before marriage because they were believed to learn crude habits and associate with bad company in the factories.[35] But there was an equally strong prejudice among working girls against domestic service, primarily because of the almost total lack of freedom involved.[36] In fact, few of the women servants surveyed by the British Women's Industrial Council at the beginning of the twentieth century had worked in industrial occupations either before becoming servants or between domestic positions.[37] Most of the female servants who were questioned in this survey had worked as dressmakers or shop assistants if they had held other jobs during their working careers.[38] It seems, therefore, that the group of individuals who became domestic servants were distinct from the group who entered industrial occupations. If this was true, then the question of mentality or motivation assumes even greater importance.

Though admittedly we are entering an impressionistic realm, the aggregate behaviour of servants suggests that some of the advantages of service, both economic and non-economic, were realised by those who accepted domestic positions and can be partially explained by this realisation, as will be examined in the succeeding chapter. Certainly, as we will later explain, when the economic advantages of service began to wane, the number of servants also diminished.

The intriguing pattern of high geographical mobility among domestics and a consistently ample supply of domestic labour at least until 1880 brings the explanation of the nature of domestic service down to the level of individual experience. The need to escape the poverty of marginal agricultural areas or overpopulated working-class homes combined with traditional patterns for lower-class employment to produce a situation that was no longer purely traditional. Because service facilitated urban migration, entry into domestic service, in spite of its traditional aspects, played a vital role in lower-class adaptation to modern urban society. We can now begin to deal with a further factor. However traditional its base, servanthood, chosen over factory work, not to mention agricultural labour, could be an extremely rational economic choice; so possibly the girls who went off to the distant cities were better calculators than their peers. In more urbanised settings, most typically in England, very young girls were set to similar choices, and again we do not have to assume that they were stupid in their decision for servanthood over other kinds of employment, particularly at a young age. But *generally* urban girls, reaching the age of twenty or so, avoided servanthood despite its advantages. This is why rural recruitment, or the solicitation of very young recruits in England, was so vital. The choice was sensible, but only if one preserved certain values of dependence that the city did not breed. Hence the older urban girl was a rarity in the servant population. This boded ill for the long-range future of servanthood, as societies became more urbanised and options more abundant. The whole recruitment pattern raises the question of what one might get out of domestic service. The occupation was not simply a haven from starvation in a rural backwater or urban slum, for it involved an economically rational choice and a number of advantages.

3. HARSH CONDITIONS AND HIGH WAGES

Any simple concept of the cause of the massive urban migration which preceded and accompanied the first stages of industrialisation is impossible to sustain. An adequate explanation must take into account both urban attraction and rural impoverishment. On the one hand, the countryside emptied out because the land could not support the sons and daughters of marginal tenant farmers. On the other hand, the cities drew many individuals who believed they would find better jobs and a more pleasant life there. In many cases, there was little real choice between starvation and migration, yet often the advantages of the cities proved to be illusory, and both the cost of living and the mortality rate were much higher in the urban centres.

Many of the young men and women who entered domestic service in the cities were impelled by a combination of factors which involved both 'push' and 'pull'. Some had no choice because agricultural work was not a viable option for them. The migration patterns described in the preceding chapter, however, clearly imply that some choice was being exercised by many migrants between some kind of industrial work and domestic service. Why, for example, did the emigrants from the Alpine regions migrate to Lyons or to Paris to serve as domestics when the concentration of industry in and around Lyons offered an equal opportunity for employment? Many of these urban immigrants must have been making a deliberate choice for the advantages which domestic service seemed to offer them.

Many young servants were probably attracted by the apparent advantages of domestic service in the cities, such as the higher wages. William Taylor, an English footman, obviously recognised the opportunity in domestic service: 'There is money to be made in service, but the person must be lucky enough to get in good places and begin service when very young.'[1] The wages of the servants in London and Paris were sufficiently attractive to draw into the cities an increasingly larger segment of the total servant population. Other servants were perhaps seduced by the various attractions of the city itself but recognised the advantages of free lodging and board in domestic service.[2] A domestic position also promised protection to the young woman separated from her family and wary of the dangers of urban life. Positions were plentiful especially if one were not too particular about the kind of situation. No special training was required; for although prior experience was often preferred, employers were generally pleased to hire any respectable candidate. Moreover, for the increasing number of women in service, domestic positions offered a more personal work experience, which they seemed to prefer over the greater freedom of factory work.

Some of these advantages turned out to be illusory, except for the tangible rewards of their compensation. A servant had almost no need and little opportunity to spend his salary, so that servants were able to amass considerable savings. This chance to save enough money to return to the country or to marry in relative comfort made domestic service an attractive alternative to the declining opportunities in agriculture, or to domestic industry or factory work. Hence the promise of some social mobility may have exercised a significant pull on the young peasants who entered the cities by the thousand and offered their services to middle- and upper-class households, but the bleak conditions of the average servant's life meant that it was no easy path to a better life.

Poor conditions for the servant in the middle-class household were due above all to the costs which his or her employment imposed upon the middle-class budget. Obviously, the middle classes were trying to acquire the attributes of a new status before they had the means to live comfortably at the new level. Money wages were only a fraction of the financial burden which employment of a servant imposed upon an employer. In the broadest sense, the servant's 'wages' included the master's responsibility to provide food and lodging even when the servant was not lodged in the same building. The expense of rent, fuel, and food could represent a sizeable percentage of the middle-class family's budget.

English commentators were much more interested than the French in calculating the costs of the material aspects of middle-class life and considerably more voluble on the questions of middle-class incomes. Consequently, one has a clearer sense of what servant employment meant to the English middle-class budget than to the French. English manuals nearly always included estimates of the costs of servants or the minimum income level at which one could expect to employ a servant. They typically suggest that for every £200 of income per year, a family could employ one female servant.[3] Since male servants' wages were about double those of females, the family income level had to reach at least £600 a year before a man could be employed.[4] But wages were only a part of the total cost of a servant. Families could expect to spend a minimum of 12 per cent of their total income on wages and the costs of servants' food and lodging.[5]

These living expenses were the most substantial elements in the cost of keeping a servant and nearly always exceeded the cost of wages. When an urban middle-class family was renting an apartment and had to rent separate rooms for their servants, this cost could be very heavy. English middle-class families were more likely to live in town houses or vertical flats so that servants were housed within the house or apartment; and the separate costs for servants were primarily for heat, electricity, and the expenses of furnishing the rooms in the attic and cellar. French middle-class families, however, generally rented single-floor apartments and for them space was at a premium. As an example, in Lyons in 1820, the rents of families employing a servant in the second *arrondissement* (the centre of the city) ranged from 125 francs to 1,500 francs, with an average of 313 francs.[6] Separate single rooms of three male servants who lived in the same area with their wives rented for 55,75 and 100 francs.[7] Thus, the addition of the rent of a separate room for a servant could substantially increase the family's expenditure on rent, which between 1870 and 1910 represented about 15 per cent of the average French middle-class budget.[8] Food costs for a servant were also substantial. An evaluation of the annual expenditure on food for a French servant in 1913 cited 588 francs as an average;[9] hence, the expenditure for food alone represented more than the average annual wage of a maid-of-all-work. Similarly, an English servant cost an employer only about £10 to £20 in wages, but the cost of feeding her was £30 per year according to one estimate.[10] Rowntree's study of York concluded that a servant cost £20 in board in 1903.[11] Unfortunately, a thrifty employer sometimes attempted to economise on these aspects of his financial responsibilities, leading to alarming abuses in providing decent housing and a proper diet for servants.

The most 'visible' problem was servants' housing. The typical servant lodging in Haussmann's Paris was the 'sixième étage' — the so-called sixth floor, actually the last floor under the mansarded roof of a large apartment block. Close enough to their employers' apartments on the floors below, the servants were segregated into a society of their own where they need not be seen but could be easily summoned.[12] In English houses, it was customary to put the female servants in attic rooms, but male servants were housed in the cellar near the kitchen and 'servants' hall'.[13] Whether the servant was housed on the sixth floor in the attic, cellar or kitchen, conditions of servant housing attracted considerable criticism.

The servant's room was generally small, with sloping ceilings, dark, poorly ventilated, unheated, dirty, lacking privacy or even safety. As a young servant in a new position, Yvonne Cretté-Breton described her dismal bedchamber with its peeling wall-paper, dirty from the smoke of fires, with only a small iron bed and no other furnishings.[14] Yet even this was better than Cretté-Breton's first job in which she had to share a bed with an older servant.[15] When servants' rooms were under the roof, they were stifling in the summer and icy cold in the winter.[16] The only window often opened on to a tiny enclosed courtyard, and the rooms were rarely adequately ventilated or lighted.[17]

The household manuals expressed concern over the usual conditions of servants' rooms and emphasised two dangers: a health hazard and an invitation to sexual promiscuity among the servants housed so closely together. The French custom of relegating servants, both male and

51

female, to the sixth floor in crowded rooms resulted in 'induced promiscuity', according to one French doctor.[18] A servant's letter to the Minister of Labour in 1913 complained of the crowded conditions among her thirty-five companions in her building's 'sixième'.[19] The English custom of separating male and female servants between the cellar and the attic apparently calmed employers' fears in this regard.

Besides the type of servants' lodgings in the 'sixième' or cellar, there were several kinds of servants who were lodged close to the families they served. Wet nurses and governesses tended to share the room of the child for whom they cared, since it was more practical to have the child's nurse close enough to respond to his cries.[20] The children's rooms were generally cleaner, better heated, and healthier than servants' rooms, but the servant who slept there lost what little privacy or independence a separate room afforded. A lady's maid sometimes slept in a room just off her mistress's bedroom. Single women saw this as a safety precaution; but this kind of arrangement failed in the case of a Parisian woman who was the victim in a sensational murder in 1887 and whose maid died with her.[21] Some individuals preferred the safety and convenience of being able to summon a servant quickly over the desire for the 'invisibility' of their servants.

In poorer households, servants fared even worse than those who were housed in the attic or cellar. Because the rental of a separate room was prohibitive for many middle-class families, the servant was given only a bed in the corner of a kitchen or in a corridor.[22] Though not exclusively a French problem, the question of space was most critical for French servant-employers. In the second *arrondissement* of Lyons in 1820, 60 per cent of the families who employed one servant rented only three rooms.[23] Thus, most servants were almost certainly housed in crowded conditions, sleeping in corridors or kitchens or sharing small servants' quarters. Even in the more affluent households which employed two or more servants, servants generally slept two or three to a room.

Conditions in the makeshift lodgings of kitchens or corridors were obviously unhealthy, with poor ventilation and no heat. Even when the kitchen was not the sleeping chamber of the servant, however, this room was his or her residence for most of the long workday. The kitchen often had the worst hygienic conditions of any room in the house or apartment.[24] In the mid-nineteenth century, kitchens were built around huge cooking stoves: 'The English kitchen was still dominated by a dirty, inefficient, labour-making, fuel-devouring monster that made the place unbearable in hot weather.'[25] Most kitchens were badly ventilated and had windows which either had to be left open summer and winter in order to clear the air of food odours or which could not be opened at all.[26] Investigators into unhealthy living conditions in Paris and London (who were often doctors), remarked upon the shocking conditions in luxurious buildings in which the kitchens were so dark that the gas had to remain on all day.[27] One French doctor argued that the combination of a day spent in a kitchen lacking light and ventilation and a night spent under the eaves in a dirty room, either too hot or too cold, was certain to cause a deterioration of the servant's strength, anaemia, and eventually tuberculosis.[28] Reformers seemed to worry particularly over the health of young servants 'scarcely acclimated to the city, accustomed to the pure air of the countryside', who were forced to work in such unhealthy surroundings.[29] They mentioned the strong possibility of contracting tuberculosis or typhoid fever under such conditions.[30] The lack of comfort in these rooms was not a matter of concern for employers, but the prospect that servants might infect the families for whom they worked eventually was recognised as a critical problem.[31]

A diagnosis of the problems involved in contemporary servants' lodgings was presented by a municipal commission on unhealthy lodgings in Paris published in 1866. The report described the lack of ventilation or of insulation which produced 'insupportable conditions'.[32] About the same time, Florence Nightingale was attempting to raise English awareness of the dangers due to unhealthy conditions in servants' rooms.[33] In spite of this early diagnosis, however, it was a long time before cures were systematically applied. A major exhibit at the Exposition on Tuberculosis in 1908 in Paris which caught the attention of English reformers,[34] described the situation which still existed. The exhibit placed two rooms side by side: one was an attic room with well-used carpet, dirty bed and walls covered with dirty, peeling paper; the other was the cell of a detainee in the prison at Fresnes, recently constructed, antiseptically clean, with electric lighting and a large window.[35] The employers who housed their servants in the former kind of room could hardly have missed the point.

Employers, however, were slow to remedy the problems of servant housing and there was no legal compulsion for them to do so, as a report to the Parisian municipal council noted.

> Servants attached to personal service are excluded from the laws protecting workers and there exist no specific rules which concern their lodgings. The housing administration does not recognise servants' rooms [within their jurisdiction].[36]

A law regulating unhealthy housing conditions passed by the municipal council of Paris in 1902 did not extend to servant housing.[37] A campaign to encourage voluntary acquiescence to minimum standards in housing conditions for servants was begun in Paris in 1905 by the *Bulletin des ligues sociales d'acheteurs* since conditions were clearly worsening under the impact of a housing shortage in Paris at the turn of the twentieth century. The league published a 'liste blanche' of buildings which met essential criteria in order to encourage construction of housing which conformed to the standards.[38] In London, legislation was finally passed in 1909 which regulated standards for underground bedrooms in regard to lighting, ventilation, and dampness.[39]

Unhealthy conditions persisted, despite some expressed concern over their effects, because the employer class was unwilling to apply an extensive remedy. Caught in the squeeze of inflation, the middle-class employer was sometimes genuinely unable to provide better quarters for his servants. Employers' social consciences were limited by the real problems of living in a town house or urban apartment without running water and heated by numerous coal-burning stoves. The standard London house of the 1860s 'was meant for the growing prosperous middle- or upper-middle-class family, with at least one servant to toil up and down its extravagant stairwell at the call of a bell, carrying buckets of coal, cans of water, and trays of food.'[40] Other explanations besides thriftiness, however, have been suggested for the maltreatment of servants by their masters. One French woman described how she had been shocked to see a mistress bake a crude, black bread for her servant rather than allow the servant to share their white bread. The mistress responded that it was necessary that servants be made to 'feel all the distance that is between them and us.'[41] This crass assertion of social superiority probably characterised only a minority of employers but subtler echoes of the attitude can be found more widely. Certainly the burdensome cost of a servant affected virtually all middle-class employers, and until legal surveillance compelled them to meet minimum standards in servant housing, the employer class tried to ignore the problem.

But servants' own complaints focused not on overcrowded rooms, to which lower-class servants were well accustomed, but on the quality of their diet. Middle-class employers were very conscious of the expense of food in a household budget. As another example of the stress on housekeeping efficiency, Madame Pariset suggested to her readers that a means of economising on food and of assuring a high level of energy in their servants was to insist that servants abandon the Parisian custom of taking *café au lait* in the morning. Pariset suggested that the mistress substitute a ten o'clock breakfast of soup made from the meat left over from the previous night so that the servant would have sufficient energy to work until five o'clock without stopping, and the mistress could save the expense of the purchase of extra coffee.[42] Although the manuals' writers advised that the servant be fed essentially the same diet as the master and mistress,[43] the diet of servants was generally much more parsimonious. Servants often complained of positions where 'the bread is doled out by the piece, and the milk by the drop' or where 'the meat was cut as if for a cat.'[44] In one case where a Parisian maid was accused of theft, she defended herself by arguing that she had been forced to steal by the cheapness of her employers and the judge treated her leniently.[45] It is difficult to generalise from servant complaints about the quality of the diet most received, though there is sufficient evidence of many employers who were less than generous. On the other hand, Charles Booth concluded in his study of London's domestic servants that

> The quality of food given to domestic servants, no doubt, depends on the liberality of the management, but is usually very good, and in all but very rare cases greatly superior to that obtainable by the other members of the working-class families from which servants are drawn. . .[46]

Servants' complaints probably stemmed from their comparison of their own diets with those of their employers and they felt aggrieved, even though they were almost certainly better off than most working-class families. And although some employers mistreated their servants, the security of servants' food and lodging was one of the great advantages of service.[47]

The workday of the servant was one of the least attractive features of domestic service since it was always long and arduous. A Parisian chambermaid complained that she was not allowed to spend any time out during a workday which lasted from 5 a.m. until 11 p.m., except for a few hours on Sunday in which to visit her child.[48] Rising at six or before ('those who would thrive, must rise by five'),[49] a domestic was required to light the fires, prepare breakfast, clean the clothing and shoes of her masters, shop for provisions, and prepare a mid-day meal by noon. If there were children in the family and no nursery maid, the domestic also had to awaken the children, feed and dress them in the morning. Afternoons were spent cleaning, washing clothing, doing some sewing, and preparing the evening meal. If the servant were employed by a master and mistress who went out in the evening or who entertained often, the servant would be up until after midnight.[50] Then, arising early the next morning, the servant began her work all over again.

The average servant worked fifteen to eighteen hours per day.[51] In 1906, a French association of servants attempted to have the servant's workday limited to fifteen hours, at a time when the average for other workers was already down to ten.[52] In fact, a common demand of servants was for a clearer definition of their workday and of their responsibilities.[53] There was a great need for some time off during the day or at least each week.[54] Sunday was generally considered a partial holiday for servants, but servants complained of being forced to work until four or five o'clock in the afternoon when they had finished a full day's work before being allowed to go out.[55] English servants generally received one day off a month in addition to the half-days on Sundays.[56] Some employers abused their servants by demanding that they work steadily through uninterrupted weeks. One Parisian servant complained in 1911 that she had received no days off and no evening out in the eight to nine months she had worked for her employer.[57] Another French servant expressed her resentment toward employers who refused to allow her any holidays.

> I am a servant of two teachers who have two days off a week, twelve days of holiday at Easter, about four months or more of summer vacation; but I am given only a half-day every five weeks, and if I ask to go out for another time apart from that, they begin to talk about firing me . . .I don't know why some employers treat their servants like serfs.[58]

And a servant's mother pleaded for better treatment for her daughter who had been in service six months without a day off: '. . . all I can say is that this woman is mistreating my daughter . . . My daughter rises at 5.30 a.m. and retires at 11 p.m.; it seems to me that I cannot leave my daughter, aged seventeen and a half, in that house.'[59] These complaints provide clear, though fragmentary, evidence that compared to other workers, the domestic servant was overworked and had much less free time.

Even the small amount of leisure time which servants enjoyed could not always be spent with friends. Since opportunities to go out in the evening were rare, their contacts with other workers were limited. As English footman William Taylor complained, 'a servant is shut up like a bird in a cage.'[60] Nor was the servant often allowed to receive friends in her employer's house.[61] A servant's social contacts were confined to acquaintances she made while doing shopping or running errands for her mistress, and to the young soldiers or artisans she met on Sundays in the parks or cafés.

The lack of free time also had a deleterious effect on the servant's family life, since the servant could spend only a few hours a week away from the employer's household.[62] Even 'maternity leave' could be very short. Henriette, the cook of François de Neufchâteau in 1827, served dinner on the 18th of January before retiring and delivering her baby about midnight. Henriette was back at work a week later.[63] In fact, because of the schedule required of domestics, except for the occasional young women who continued in service in order to support a child who was in the care of a nurse, most servants either never married or left service when they married.

A survey of the deplorable working conditions of most servants can make it difficult to understand why urban immigrants continued to enter service until the early twentieth century. We return here to the central problem of 'push' and 'pull', not only to explain why people entered service but also why people who had some choice remained in service for a certain period. The choice of domestic service over some other kind of work demonstrates that service must have been sufficiently attractive to an important segment of the rural emigrants to counteract the disadvantages of virtual loss of freedom, long hours, and frequent mistreatment. To be sure, the traditional character of domestic service, particularly for women, had a significant influence on the decision. And most individuals never had a wide variety of options. Above all, however, the relatively high level of servants' compensation provided an effective motivation in the face of harsh conditions and virtual bondage. The fact that servants were able to accumulate savings is an indication of the real advantage which they enjoyed over the rest of the working classes; 'lodged and fed, often clothed, they could accumulate savings, that the worker burdened with a family, found it difficult to amass.'[64]

Servants' wages were governed by a variety of conventions which expanded the value of the monetary wage. The salary of the servant seemed low because it did not include the value of the servant's food and lodging. In addition, there were a number of gratuities which both the employer and the servant had come to expect was a part of the contract for service. In eighteenth-century England, a large part of the income of servants in large households were vails, the fees collected from the guests of the house.[65] A guest in an aristocratic household, upon leaving, was expected to bestow a gift on each servant according to the rank of the servant and his own generosity. The practice became so annoying to both employers and guests that English employers formed an organised movement to abolish vails-giving.[66] But in spite of the campaign against vails, the practice persisted in the nineteenth century, though only in very large households.[67] Other payments also were considered servant perquisites, such as the money paid to a servant who set out fresh decks of cards when guests were playing cards in the employer's house.[68] Finally, in England, as in France, there was the custom of merchants who paid commissions to the servants of their regular customers or who gave the servants Christmas boxes. The perquisites could represent a substantial increment to the servant's wages, but they were obviously more common in the very large households of aristocratic and upper-middle-class families, and were not significant for most servants of middle-class households.

In France there were a great variety of servant perquisites. First, was the 'arrhes' or 'denier à Dieu', an amount paid to the newly-hired servant to seal the contract. Examples of the practice can be found in account books of both aristocratic and middle-class households in the nineteenth century. François de Neufchâteau hired a servant in 1822 to whom he paid a fee of 5 francs plus her first month's wages of 25 francs.[69] Marie Vinquet received her 'denier à Dieu' only after four months of service with Dr Créquy in 1838 along with payment of four months' wages.[70] Another resident of the Ardennes like Dr Créquy, Madame Vermon, paid a new servant 5 francs in 1836 when she hired her.[71] The servant could keep this fee if he or she left soon after being hired.

New servants were also often reimbursed for their trip to the home of the employer if arrangements for hiring had been made before the servant relocated. *The Servant's Practical Guide* mentioned this custom in 1880,[72] and accounts of a Parisian widow note payment of a 'denier à Dieu' and travel expenses in 1871 of 5 francs and 7 francs respectively.[73] Travel expenses were always expected when a wet nurse was hired to come to the home of an employer.[74]

Besides the one-time gifts or perquisites, there were several important annual or continuing payments to servants. Both in France and in England, the servant's monetary wage was supplemented by a customary payment for wine or beer. Traditionally, the master had provided his servants with wine or beer as part of their food allotment, and there was generally a pre-determined amount of wine or beer set aside for each servant. In the nineteenth century this custom was gradually commuted to a monetary payment.[75] In France, by the turn of the twentieth century, the wine allowance was clearly stated in job offers as part of the wage; for example, *Le Serviteur* on April 14, 1908 carried offers of positions for eight valets for 120 to 160 francs per month 'plus wine', and for twenty-one maids-of-all-work for 45 to 50 francs per month 'plus 10 francs for wine'. The wine allowance had thus become a considerable bonus when added to the monthly wage. In England, the beer money was usually calculated in the cost of 'board wages', which also included a certain amount of tea and soap per month for each domestic.[76] The amount which an English servant might receive in this way varied widely according to local custom.[77]

An annual gift which was traditional in France was the New Year's 'étrennes'. Madame Vermon's maid received only 3 francs as 'étrennes' in 1830 but her wages were only 8 francs per month.[78] More common was the case of a maid-of-all-work in the Puy-de-Dôme in 1843, who earned 70 francs a year and received 15 francs for 'étrennes'.[79] At the New Year in 1872 a Parisian widow gave each of her five servants gifts ranging from 20 to 35 francs.[80] 'Étrennes' were also sometimes paid to the servants of close friends or relatives who had performed some special service.[81] Unlike vails-giving in England, the offering of gratuities to another individual's servant was rare in France, except for the 'étrennes'.

In England, an annual gift to one's servant was generally made at Christmas. Such gifts could be either monetary ones or gifts of clothing or useful items, or perhaps a combination of the two. Margaret Powell, in recounting her experiences of Christmases in service, recalls that the gifts she received were nearly always useful, 'print dress lengths, aprons, black stockings, not silk of course, they never gave you anything frivolous.'[82] Obviously, such gift-giving depended upon the relationship between a particular servant and his or her employer, so that any generalisation is risky, but gifts of some kind at Christmas were expected.

Less important than the monetary gratuities, but common in practice were several non-monetary perquisites. One of these perquisites was the cast-off clothing of the master and mistress. The quantity and quality of the clothing depended on the income level of the employer, although most commentators indicated that 'it goes without saying that real jewellry and furs are never given' to a servant.[83] Cast-off clothing was probably a valuable perquisite only for servants of very wealthy employers, since an English servant complained in 1894 that there was not 'one place in a hundred where the servant gets any of his master's clothes.'[84] Middle-class employers were also more likely to be concerned about encouraging servants' vanity if they gave them their cast-off clothing.[85]

Although customs varied widely, servants, particularly male servants, often received some articles of clothing from their employers. Liveried male servants received their uniforms, but also some wealthy employers outfitted their servants once a year or at the time of hiring.[86] And most contracts for service included the care of the laundry of servants since most employers were concerned that their domestics should at least be reasonably clean.[87]

Moreover, there were incidental perquisites which accrued to certain positions. The cook was particularly favoured because of her right to sell the 'cooking fats and the ashes' for whatever this was worth.[88] More important, the cook purchased the household provisions and her contacts with shopkeepers could obtain substantial gratuities for her. A common and often deplored practice was the system of commissions or kickbacks to servants paid by shopkeepers. Called 'poundage' in England and 'sou pour livre' in France, this practice reached astonishing proportions in the nineteenth century.[89] Despite the prohibitions of mistresses and the threats that this practice was illegal, few servants were ever prosecuted for this kind of 'domestic theft'. The servant who purchased the provisions for a large household could add noticeably to her wages and to her savings; the story was told of a French cook who earned only 400 francs a year but who was able to put 1,000 francs a year into her savings account.[90] Some mistresses were kept unaware of the practice by a clever cook who fed the other servants inferior or spoiled food, and added the difference to her savings. Lavinia Swainbank, in recalling such an experience while she was a kitchenmaid, commented that 'the cook always had her perks from the various tradesmen, and ours was no exception.'[91]

Finally, there are scattered references to other gifts to servants. Bequests in an employer's will have already been mentioned. Some employers also provided servants with a retirement income, such as the Galliffet family of France who made payments on pensions every year between 1818 and 1830, as listed in their household accounts.[92] An occasion such as the marriage of two servants might also inspire an employer to be generous. This is what happened when two servants of François de Neufchâteau were married in 1826.[93] But these gifts depended completely on the closeness of the relationship between an individual servant and his or her employer and they could not be expected as perquisites of the occupation.

The monetary wage of the servant was subject to infinite variations according to the income level of the employer, the qualifications of the servant, and local custom, so that it is very difficult to estimate the 'average' wage. For Paris, where the disparity of incomes was greatest, the *Statistique générale* of prices and salaries in 1853 simply conceded the impossibility of formulating an average servant's wage.[94] But a general evaluation of servants' wages in Paris over the long run can and has been made.[95] Expressed graphically, these figures clearly reveal the trend of wages in the course of the century and the disparity between the average male servant's wage and the wage of the maid-of-all-work. French wages increased rapidly in the 1840s and 1850s, but the greatest increase came in the 1870s, after which they tended to level off (Fig. 3.1). After 1880, French wage levels tended to stagnate and servants gradually lost their advantage in this regard.

Wages outside of Paris were consistently lower reflecting the lower cost of living in the provincial cities. Thus, for example, the average male servant in Toulouse in 1853 earned 252 francs per year and the female 180 francs; in Nancy the male servant earned 300 francs and the female 252 francs.[96] In Paris, the average valet received 720 francs in 1853 and the female domestic earned approximately 390 francs.[97] A male servant earned 2½ to 3 times as much in Paris as in other cities while a female might earn up to twice as much in Paris as elsewhere. But in the provinces, as in Paris, wages rose rapidly until about 1880 when they levelled off.

The trend in English wages in the nineteenth century is less easily established since the wage data are not available for a continuous series, but some indications of the trend can be obtained by comparing a variety of wage estimates from 1824-25 and 1883. Table 3.2 shows the estimated increase in female servants' wages over this period as 59 per cent. A comparison of this increase to other female workers' wages shows that servants were keeping pace with the general increase in female wages. Over the same period, French servants' wages were rising on an average of 100 to 150 per cent, but French servants' wages kept pace with other French female workers' wages only until about 1880.

As in France, English male servants were the élite of domestic service, earning far more than females with equivalent experience. Average wages for English butlers about the turn of the century were £58 6s. per year; for footmen, £26 7s.; and for other male servants, £38 6s. per year.[98] Average annual wages for a general female servant at the same time was £14 9s.; for cooks, the average wage was between £16 and £24, depending on age and experience; for parlourmaids,

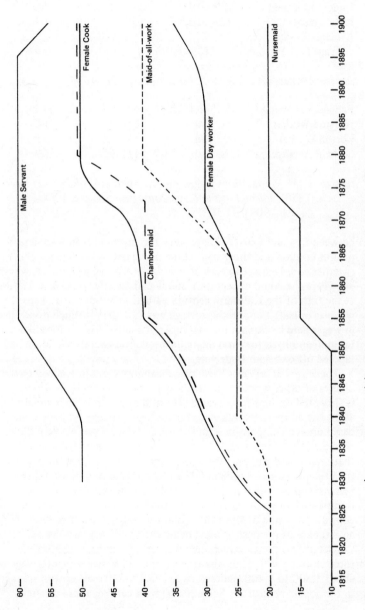

Source: Gustav Bienaymé, *Journal de la Société de Statistique de Paris*, XL (November, 1899), pp.366-85.

Table 3.1: Increase in female wages in England, 1824 – 1883

	1824 – 1825	1883	% Increase
Housemaid or parlourmaid	£10 –16/year	£15 –25/year	54%
Underhousemaid	£ 8 –10	£12 –16	56
Lady's maid	£14 –16	£20 –30	67
Average Servant Wage (Est.)	£12	£19	59

Source: Parkes, p.125; Beeton, p.8; James, p.126.

Female Silk Worker	5s./week	10s. 9d./week	118%
Worsted Worker	6s. 11d.	11s. 0d.	80
Cotton Worker	8s. 10d.	13s. 4d.	65
General Average	7s. 5d.	11s. 9d.	59

Source: G. H. Wood, 'Real Wages and the Standard of Comfort since
        1850', *Journal of the Royal Statistical Society*, LXXII
        (March 1909), 91-103.

between £14 and £20.[99] There were also differences in wage levels
paid in London and those paid in the provinces. A housemaid in her
twenties could expect to earn an average of £17 5s. in London, whereas
elsewhere she could expect only about £16 2s.[100] A cook in London
at the turn of the twentieth century earned an average of £21 8s.,
whereas outside London the average was £20 2s.[101] Such disparities
in wages help to explain the enormous attractiveness of cities like
London and Paris for rural migrants, even after overall migration had
tapered off or begun to decline.

The wages of servants have little meaning except in relation to the
salaries of other workers, particularly in those occupations which
represented options for servants. The author of a French manual from
1904 argued that servants' wages made a good salary for a woman,
based upon a comparison with the wages earned by a female millinery
worker.[102] An investigation of English servants actually recognised
that their board pay plus their wages made their compensation greater
than that of factory workers,[103] and such realisation must explain why
many servants 'chose' to be servants despite the many drawbacks of the
occupation. Any comparison of servants' wages and other salaries must
consider the value of a servant's food and lodging. In Paris about 1883
an estimate of the cost of basic living expenses for a Parisian worker
was set at 850 francs, which included rent, food, heat, lighting and
some clothing.[104] Thus, the true value of a Parisian servant's wage was
about 1,300 to 1,400 francs per year. In 1885, female cotton spinners
in the department of the Seine (Paris) were earning approximately

780 francs per year; males, aged 15 to 21, approximately 930 francs; and adult males, 1,650 francs.[105] The Parisian male servant, whose monetary wage was about 720 francs, was receiving compensation of slightly less than 1,600 francs or somewhat lower than the cotton spinner. Moreover, the servant worked a longer average day so that the per hour value of his work was much lower than that of the factory worker. Thus, while service was a profitable occupation for a young Frenchman, when he reached his majority, he could earn a higher wage in industry. While other male wages continued to rise after 1880, the wage of male servants remained remarkably stable. This factor can explain much of the exodus of men from service in the nineteenth century and the acceleration of the feminisation of service between 1880 and 1914.

The female servant, on the other hand, earned a wage which the female cotton spinner could not match. The female servant's wage was worth over 1,300 francs, compared to the cotton spinner's wage of 780 francs. Female servants worked a longer day, about 15 to 18 hours, compared to the 10 or 11-hour day of the cotton spinner, yet even with this difference, the compensation of the servant per hour was greater. It is true that it becomes increasingly misleading to compare servants' wages with those of a cotton spinner, since the latter occupation was not one of the best options for women in the 1880s. Instead, silk spinning was becoming an increasingly important source of feminine employment and female silk workers' wages were rising twice as fast as those of cotton workers. The differences in wages reflect the changing nature of women's employment toward the end of the nineteenth century of which the decline in domestic servants was one aspect. For, as female wages were rising in some industrial and service sectors, female domestic servants' wages were levelling off, as had those of male domestics, after 1880 (see Fig. 3.2). Just at the time when some employment opportunities for women were widening, the domestic servants' advantageous economic position was eroding.

English servants, like the French, also earned only half of their compensation in the form of monetary wages. Lodging and board represented about one-half of the total average compensation of a male servant and approximately two-thirds for a female servant. Thus, an average maid-of-all-work in England at the end of the nineteenth century was earning approximately £45, including 'board wages'. Female silk workers at the same time were earning somewhat more than ten shillings per week, or about £24 to £25 per year.[106] A study of the earnings of semi-skilled women in 1906 produced the following comparison:[107]

Cotton frame tenters	£50
Clothing machinists	34
Shop assistants	50

Engineering machine operators	32
Laundresses	30
Domestic servants	49

It is clear that domestic servants were continuing to do comparatively well even at the beginning of the twentieth century. In addition, time lost often cut seriously into the annual income of a worker, while it played a negligible role in domestic work. Industrial slowdowns, unemployment and illness were more likely to cut into the wages of the worker than the servant. In spite of the longer working hours, then, domestic service offered a distinct monetary advantage over other kinds of female employment in the nineteenth century.

A less favourable aspect of domestic servants' wages, however, was their trend during the course of an individual career. In the case of English servants, according to Charles Booth, the custom was either to hire at a relatively good wage and then maintain that wage through years of service or to hire at a low wage and increase it after a year or so, if the servant proved to be a valuable worker.[108] Thus it is not surprising that servant's wages when seen on an individual level show remarkable stability. Family accounts from France indicate that wages of individual servants who remained in service for years did not improve significantly, although these servants' perquisites may have improved after years of faithful service. Because service for the individual was an important transitional phase, in which the turnover in positions was very high, the general curve of wages shows an increasingly higher wage for older, and presumably more experienced, servants until the wage levels peak about the age of thirty-five and begin to decline. Servants were constantly changing positions in order to better themselves, and wages were rising at least until 1880 in order to attract young men and women into the occupation. But after a certain age was reached, length of service no longer was accompanied by increases in wages, so that as the servant population aged or remained permanent the wages also stabilised.[109] This individual experience may account for part of the stabilisation of servants' wage levels after 1880 since the servant population was beginning to age as more servants remained in service permanently after 1880 and there were fewer new recruits entering service.

More generally, the trend of individual servants' wages (not overall rates over time) introduces one of several analytical puzzles in discussing the conditions of service. Clearly those unfortunate enough to have to remain in service permanently would not benefit with age and experience past a rather early point, though it might be noted that factory workers encountered a similar age-wage relationship. What is more interesting is the problem of wages before thirty-five. They rose in part because of experience, but in part also because, as we will see, servants were constantly tempted to quit servanthood or at least quit

Fig. 3.2: Index of female salaries in Paris, 1850-1910. Base: 100 in 1900

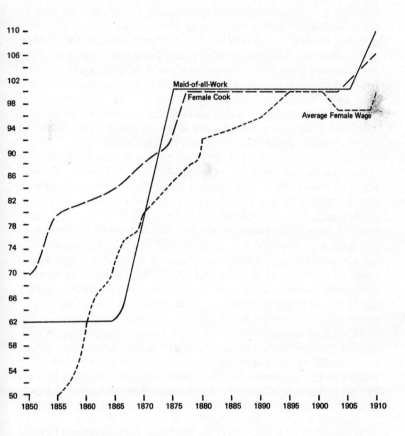

Maid-of-all-Work

Female Cook

Average Female Wage

Source: Jeanne Singer-Kérel, Le Coût de la vie à Paris de 1840 à 1954 (Paris, 1961);
Gustav Bienaymé, *Journal de la Société de Statistique de Paris,* XL
(November, 1899), 366-85.

their particular job. Was quitting, then, a function of inadequately rising wages which failed to compensate for the other problems of the servant condition? Or were servants not completely 'economic men', so that they quit despite wages that rose quickly enough to make their trade worthwhile? This is really asking what servants wanted, and probably the best answer will prove to be that they wanted servanthood and its monetary benefits — to this extent being 'economic men' — but for a limited period, after which wages would rarely compensate. And for those who saw the plight of older servants, this calculation could only appear all the more logical.

As to the more general wage trends, we can project two possible patterns for the servant choosing his or her occupation. One, with 'push' involved, stresses the traditional aspect; but this is not incompatible with pleasure at monetary prospects once the actual experience was launched. The other involves a more active choice, in which servants knew or believed in an economic advantage from the first, whether they were forced to leave home or not. These two patterns were probably complementary in many situations. The main point to stress, against an approach that would dwell on traditionalism and subjection to exploitation alone, is that a rational economic calculation could be involved. In a sense, the test of this complicated equation came only in the later nineteenth century, when the 'femina economica' began to realise that the economics of her position were changing, and began to follow the earlier pattern of the 'homo economicus'.

In England throughout the nineteenth century, the oversupply of unskilled female labour should have kept domestic wages down, since most unskilled women served as domestics at least for a short time.[110] In spite of the oversupply, however, female domestic wages in England did not suffer more than other female wages, and the English servant, like her Continental counterpart, enjoyed a considerable economic advantage throughout the century.

In labour-short France, on the other hand, the competition to employ a limited supply of servants should have forced wages up continuously. Yet, as the earlier graphs clearly indicate, French servant wages levelled off between 1880 and 1905, just as the decline in total number of servants should have pushed up wage levels. This levelling-off of servants' wages poses a very difficult problem. Part of the explanation may be the ageing of the servant population, although even after 1880 the percentage of permanent or career servants was still very small. Admittedly, the trend of Parisian servants' wages in this period paralleled the cost of living in Paris, which had risen rapidly before 1880 and which rose again after 1905. Yet the fact that competition for the declining number of servants did not push up wages suggests that the demand for servants was also waning after 1880. Although similar data are not available for England, it is clear that after 1880 the middle classes were finding it increasingly difficult to afford a servant. Members of the English middle classes were complaining in the 1870s that the cost of living had increased by 50 per cent.[111] The housing shortage in Paris caused rents to rise rapidly (an increase of 20 to 25 per cent between 1900 and 1911),[112] and aggravated the problem of providing room for servants. Fewer middle-class families in France and England could afford to satisfy their desire to employ a servant after 1880.

There is still another cause of the declining middle-class demand for servants, in addition to the weakening economic position of many middle-class families. The middle-class inclination to employ a live-in maid after 1880 was lessening. The middle classes wanted to privatise their lives and had begun to feel that live-in servants were obtrusive. This increased stress on the nuclear family was associated with declining family size. The conscious limiting of family size had begun much earlier (as early as the eighteenth century by French families), but its main effects were just beginning to be felt by the English middle classes in the mid-nineteenth century. And this in turn was clearly linked to the declining demand for servants. The decline in the demand for servants may have resulted from the economic crisis which English middle-class families faced in attempting to afford the 'paraphernalia of gentility' which were increasingly expensive, as John and Olive Banks have argued.[113] But there was also simply a diminishing need for household help to care for fewer children. And although the economic argument is highly persuasive, the motivation for this decline in demand could also have been due to a growing intimacy within the middle-class family and of a wish to be closer to and provide better care for one's children. This wish produced an increased exclusiveness by middle-class families toward outsiders,[114] and in particular, a movement to eliminate intermediaries like servants who might come between parents and children. Though we do not yet know a great deal about the evolution of middle-class family life in this period, it is clear that servants were to play a decreasing role in that life-style.

When wages became increasingly disadvantageous for male servants and began to offer less of an advantage to female domestics, important symptoms of dissatisfaction among servants became more frequent, associations of servants were established in increasing numbers, and the complaints of servants multiplied. Wages were not the only factor; obviously, the widening of occupational opportunities for women, particularly in the growth of white-collar occupations, added to servant dissatisfaction with the conditions of domestic service. Servants began to compare their living and working conditions with those of other workers. In addition to unpleasant working conditions, the servant lacked the limited freedom that the average worker enjoyed. The increasing level of visible dissatisfaction among servants underlines the importance of the declining economic advantages, since servants no longer felt adequately compensated for the inconveniences of service. The option to search for other employment was taken by increasing numbers of both male and female urban immigrants after 1880. Their choice left a gap in the middle-class household which was only gradually filled by modern technological conveniences.

To return to the important question of inferring mentality from the descriptions of working conditions, we should be aware that we are entering a very impressionistic realm. Descriptions of conditions, even when taken literally, can be made to sound more awful than they actually were. Coming from crowded cottages or tenements, many servants actually had more space and privacy in horrible little urban apartments than they were accustomed to – more so in England, doubtless, than in France where the space problem was so acute. Servants' diet also needs careful comparison to other elements of the lower classes, for while inferior to the masters' level, servants' diet was not necessarily lower than lower-class standards more generally. Finally, as to the most obvious horror of servant life, lack of free time, we must be wary of literal acceptance of conditions, which undeniably differentiates servants from other lower-class groups whose hours were less overwhelming. Servants did, for example, shop regularly. They did not necessarily rush home for their next chore. They might stop to chat with other servants or with men along the street – and this became a source of a marriage pattern with shopkeepers and artisans. Even at home servants were not constantly driven. Here much would depend on the particular mistress, and the specific situation. Servants themselves certainly recognised this fact; job-changing, in search of a better set of conditions and/or in defiance of an over-demanding mistress, was a commonplace of the occupation. None of this should downplay the real constraints in servants' conditions and the kind of choice they had to make in remaining servants, when other, freer occupations were available. But many servants found their own ways to make their life more endurable, which was no small cause of the annoyance mistresses felt in directing their servants. The ways in which many servants made servanthood more endurable may have contributed to the decision many middle-class mistresses ultimately made that trying to direct servants was more trouble than it was worth. The conditions of most servants' lives during the whole nineteenth century were the result of a tangle of motivations and economic factors. The attitudes of the employer class had an important effect on these conditions. Crass social snobbery suggests one reason for the mistreatment of servants, but more important was the haste of the middle classes to buttress their newly-acquired social status by the employment of a servant whom they could not comfortably afford. To be sure, abstract values reflected the reality of the hardships of this new middle class, hindered by the very slow increases in technology and social services. The necessity to carry coal, shop daily for provisions, heat stoves, and keep themselves clean without the benefit of running water was solved at the expense of the servant class. While domestic labour was relatively plentiful and cheap, servants were used to take up the slack in the evolution of household technology.

The weakness of servant dissent undoubtedly exacerbated the mistreatment of servants by encouraging employers to continue to take advantage of servants' relative quiescence.[115] The disorganisation of most servants can be partially attributed to the isolated character of domestic work but this does not explain the willingness of the majority of servants to continue to work in domestic positions in spite of the hardships. This willingness to work reinforces the impression that before about 1900 many servants felt adequately compensated by their wages and by the belief that domestic service offered them the chance for upward mobility and/or the fulfilment of traditional aspirations. The existence of alternative employment and the patterns of long-range migration among servants clearly demonstrate that some servants were choosing service for its advantages, some illusory and some very real. Wage levels for female servants clearly justified their choice. More important, however, were the opportunities for saving for the future and for making contacts, even if only on a Sunday afternoon walk or a shopping excursion, with individuals outside of their own class. Whether servants' faith in domestic service as a channel for social advantage was justified by the facts must be examined more thoroughly, but the fact that many young urban immigrants continued to enter this virtual servitude obviously demonstrates the strength of their belief.

4. HIRING AND FIRING

Hiring servants was 'the greatest plague of life' in the nineteenth century. If one could hire a 'good' servant at the outset, the problems of keeping domestics could, theoretically at least, be eliminated. From the servant's standpoint, if one were lucky enough to be hired by a reasonable employer, she would not need to change positions frequently and might assure herself of acceptable working conditions. Both employers and servants consequently demanded an adequate screening process as beneficial to both. This demand for an equitable system of job placement for servants was the most commonly repeated complaint in the nineteenth century, whether in middle-class journals or in the publications of servant associations.

More broadly, job placement was vitally related to the servant's reaction to the urban environment. Domestic service itself could act as a channel for urban acculturation by easing the transition from countryside to city.[1] But before this process could begin, the servant needed to be placed at least once as a servant, when he or she migrated to the city, and this experience could be traumatic. Both the formal (agencies) and the informal (personal contacts) networks for recruiting and placing servants in urban households had an important effect on facilitating the transition from the rural to the urban milieu; for the ease with which the servant could place himself and his relative job stability often determined the rate at which he could adapt to the city. At best, the channels of placement, with the background of the traditional pattern of service in the agricultural environment, could soften the impact of the migration to the city and lessen the effect of uprooting.[2] It is normally believed that people born in the city, even in the lower classes, were more likely to be upwardly mobile than low-status immigrants from the countryside.[3] But servanthood could at least reduce this differential if, through job placement and the occupation itself, the immigrant made a relatively painless transition to the urban milieu. Placement and job stability, in other words, are a vital part of the larger issues of mobility and the role of service in forming a modern urban population.

Hiring and firing also defined the occupation itself. Domestic service was a status and a condition but it was also an unskilled occupation. Whether service was simply an apprenticeship, one rung on a mobility ladder, or a permanent career or profession depended to a great extent on the hiring and firing processes and the average job stability of servants. Although servants continued to enter service in the cities in increasing numbers until 1880 or 1890, which suggests an acceptance of the conditions of service, many expressed their dissatisfaction once within the urban environment by the constant turnover in domestic positions. On the other hand, a high turnover may also indicate upward mobility. With the countryside providing a constant supply of servants to the city, it is possible that domestic positions were continually being refilled by new immigrants to the city as more experienced urban domestics moved into other jobs in the urban economy or married and left the employment market.

In addition, the hiring process was almost the only point at which the interests of servants coincided with those of the working classes in general, since most servants were isolated from their peers and were slow to recognise common interests and grievances. Employment agencies handled the placement of many categories of workers, including domestics of all kinds, so that servants' complaints and criticisms of the placement machinery involved them in a movement which had great importance for other kinds of workers as well. The problems of placement in the cities also inspired the formation of servants' unions and some attempts to link servants' associations with the general labour movement.

A basic question in the discussion of the placement mechanism concerns the supply of domestics in relation to the number of jobs available. A quantitative assessment of the supply of and demand for servants is almost impossible. The supply of women for domestic work was highly flexible and might be judged almost inexhaustible if one considers charing or temporary domestic work. Many women turned to this kind of employment in order to supplement family income and often after being deserted by husbands or widowed.[4] In England some mill girls turned to domestic service as a temporary substitute during industrial slow-downs.[5] Moreover, it is clear that the ranks of the urban servant class were constantly being swelled by a crowd of newly-arrived immigrants to the cities.[6]

The supply of servants was also carefully encouraged by employment agents because it was to their advantage to register as many servants as possible. Apart from the fee paid for registration by each servant, the profit-making agencies wanted to attract job offers from employers by a wide range of job candidates.[7] 'They attract a crowd of people to the capital where they find only misery, the number of places offered by employers through agencies being so many fewer than the number of positions sought by servants.'[8] Charges that the commercial employment agencies 'tolerated by the police' bilked both employers and servants culminated in several investigations of the situation by the French government.[9] The Parisian prefect of police, defending himself against such charges as early as 1820, admitted that to the 'detriment of the unfortunate class of unemployed servants', agencies placed 'only ten out of every hundred.'[10] An English servant articulated a similar complaint in 1894, insisting that registry offices were making considerable profit from the plight of unemployed servants.[11]

In spite of the charges, however, unemployment (by official calculations) among servants was low compared to other occupations. The only available statistics on servant employment are those collected

Table 4.1. French unemployment by occupations, 1896-1906: percentage of total in each occupation

	Males %			Females %		
	1896	1901	1906	1896	1901	1906
Agriculture	6.37	6.07	9.41	9.78	9.01	9.97
Industry	7.18	7.92	10.03	7.83	8.46	7.46
Commerce	8.44	8.74	10.35	7.94	7.93	9.96
Professions	9.62	9.68	11.27	8.49	8.82	11.32
Servants	7.37	6.93	8.60	6.86	6.71	8.49
Average	7.67	7.68	10.03	7.97	8.22	8.15

Source: *Statistique générale,* 1906, I, 3rd part, 40.

by the French government between 1896 and 1906.[12] It is clear from these data that although unemployment increased somewhat for servants during the decade, their relative position remained very good. Until the turn of the century, the demand for domestic servants remained rather consistent, and was generally in excess of the supply so that employers were willing to take almost any candidate for a domestic position.[13] Service remained a 'refuge'[14] for the unskilled urban migrants because of the relative ease with which domestic positions could be found, but in fact this ease might somewhat lessen the hardship suggested by the need for such a 'refuge'.

For until the 1880s, servants enjoyed a very favourable bargaining position in the balance of supply and demand, although precise figures on unemployment rates are lacking. The rapidly rising wages of servants from 1850 to 1880[15] suggest that the demand for servants exceeded the supply, forcing wages up dramatically. A continually replenished supply of servants who had migrated to the cities did not completely fill this demand until after 1880 when the stabilisation of wages demonstrates the altered position of servants. Although the number of servants declined, the employer class demand for servants also weakened, so that wages remained relatively constant and unemployment rose. This point at which the balance of supply and demand was tipped coincided with the regularisation of the servants' free movement in the labour market.

Both before and after this important economic watershed, the more often the servant changed positions, the more important the machinery for placement became. Obviously, however, their favourable supply position and the problems they encountered in urban life and initial exposure to middle-class discipline made job-changing a particularly important phenomenon before the 1880s. From the employer's point of view, the nineteenth-century servant was typically 'unstable',[16] constantly on the move from one position to another without stopping long enough in one household to become attached to a particular family, continually seeking better positions.[17] The domestic economy manuals emphasised that it was 'a great science to know how to acquire and keep servants'.[18] Although an English servant commented that Continental servants must be better treated because they moved about less,[19] both French and English employers gave the impression that the urban servant population was a highly mobile group, never satisfied with remaining too long in any household.

Employers' complaints imply that servants were more likely to leave of their own accord than be dismissed, and employers were reluctant to dismiss a servant except for a serious reason because finding a new servant was a 'torment' for them.[20] An employer could become very accommodating when faced with the prospect of losing a satisfactory servant, as was the experience of Margaret Powell in service in the 1920s, whose employer offered her a higher salary when she announced her intention to leave.[21] According to custom, both employer and servant were obligated to give notice before leaving or dismissal. But dismissal of a servant without notice could result from a variety of reasons, ranging from dishonesty to 'moral misconduct' to disobedience to stated orders.[22] In fact, however, in the mid-nineteenth century employers were reluctant to utilise this advantage since it left them with the unpleasant task of hiring another servant.

Upon leaving a position, an English servant always requested a 'character' or letter of reference without which it was virtually impossible to secure another position. However, employers were not required by law to give such a letter[23] and, once a servant had surrendered the letter from a previous employer, he or she could not demand that letter back.[24] As a solution, servants often forged letters so that employers could not depend upon the authenticity of such references.[25] So annoying was this problem to English employers that English legislation in 1792 and again in 1903 established the punishment for the use of a forged character as a fine of £20 and up to twelve months in jail.[26] Employers could use this power as a weapon to prevent servants from leaving or to complicate the search for another position. French servants were rather better protected in this regard because the servant had the legal right to receive a certificate which stated the length of his service and the date on which he left his employer's service without comment on his competence unless he requested it.[27] The servant was thus protected from a vindictive employer, but the new employer had no evidence of satisfactory performance of domestic duties.

In France too, letters certifying the circumstances of a servant's former position could be easily forged.[28] Thus, hiring and firing became very sensitive personal issues in the master-servant relationship.

This in turn helps to explain the exaggeration of employers' complaints, for not all servants were as peripatetic as their masters implied. Unfortunately, the length of time spent in one employer's household by an individual servant is one of the most difficult factors to trace. Some indications of job stability for French servants can be obtained from two small samples of urban neighbourhoods in Lyons and Versailles between 1866 and 1876. Both Versailles' Quartier St. Louis and Lyons' sixth *arrondissement* were wealthy areas and both indicate a considerable amount of servant stability which may not be true of less comfortable households where servants received poorer treatment.[29] In the St. Louis section of Versailles in 1876, there were 85 families, employing a total of 129 servants, who had been residents of that section since 1866.[30] Of the 129 servants employed there, 77 had served the same household for 5 years, and 12 had been employed in the same household for 10 years or more. Consequently, more than half of the servants employed in this section in 1876 had served the same family for at least 5 years and nearly 10 per cent had served in the same household for 10 years or more. Lyons' sixth *arrondissement* shows less job stability of domestics and much lower residential stability on the part of their employers.[31] There were 73 families, comprising 121 servants, who had lived in the same section between 1872 and 1876. Of the 121 servants employed there, 30 had served the same families for at least 5 years, or 25 per cent of the total in this sample. Hence, the servants in Lyons, aside from a significant minority, may have changed jobs fairly often. Even in Versailles, it is quite possible that the servants who changed positions within a five-year period may have changed jobs very frequently thus giving observers the general impression of a high turnover in domestic positions. And there is every indication that domestics in wealthier households were less likely to leave their advantageous positions than were the servants employed in meaner circumstances.

Better information is available on the average length of service of an English servant. At the end of the nineteenth century, a survey of 1,864 households in London and 2,443 households throughout England and Wales indicated that the average amount of time a servant had already spent in the same household was just over three years.[32] But the mean is misleading, for there were clearly two separate patterns operating. Of servants who had put in less than five years of service in the same house, the average period of service was just over a year. However, among the servants who had spent more than five years — about one servant in five — the average was nearly two decades with the same families. So a minority of servants fit the literary stereotype of the long-serving family retainer, while the majority of servants changed positions every year or two. As Table 4.2 demonstrates, the shortest length of time spent in a particular household is that of the general servant. Cooks, housemaids and other servants all manifested greater job stability. The reason for this fact lies in the nature of domestic service. General servants were the youngest, least experienced and least skilled of all servants. A young woman who acquired some skills would quickly move up to a more skilled position like parlourmaid or cook, either in the same household, or more likely, in a different household. The domestic who was not able to make this transition to a more skilled position was also likely to be mobile because she was continually being fired for incompetence or replaced by younger girls. The high rate of turnover in domestic positions thus points to a high rate of entry into and disappearance out of the domestic labour market. But the turnover also suggests a high level of mobility within the occupation: the more capable newcomers rather quickly acquired skills which earned them higher-paid semi-skilled positions and the less competent kept moving downward and, ultimately, out of domestic service.[33]

The high turnover in domestic positions meant that servants spent a significant part of their short careers in service seeking new positions. When a servant changed jobs, there were several means by which to find another position: municipal employment offices in France and the registry offices in England, some private commercial agencies, religious and philanthropic organisations, servants' associations (after 1875), and private contacts with employers through the merchants who supplied them or through other servants. One link with the agricultural tradition persisted in the early nineteenth century – the open-air labour market. This kind of exchange in eighteenth-century England was described by Thomas Hardy in *Far from the Madding Crowd* when shepherd Gabriel was forced to seek a job after he lost his own flock.[34] In nineteenth-century Orléans on the second day in November and on the feast of St John (June 24), domestics gathered in the market square and employers selected those whom they wanted to hire.[35] Although intended primarily for agricultural 'domestics', these gatherings also included household servants. Similar labour markets could be found throughout France early in the nineteenth century.[36] But such methods of hiring were exceptional in the experience of most urban servants in the nineteenth century.

The most common means of obtaining employment was by recommending oneself to bakers, grocers and butchers since 'when in need of a servant, the mistress, or her housekeeper, asks different merchants.'[37] An employer also sought domestics through friends and acquaintances.[38] These personal contacts were preferred by employers because they mistrusted agencies and disliked the fees which agents exacted for their services.[39] Moreover, obtaining a servant through one's trusted friends helped to eliminate the uncertainty in

Table 4.2. Length of service of English domestics

	London		England and Wales (Excluding London)	
Number of servants in survey	1,864		2,443	
Servants who at time of survey had been in same household for		%		%
Under 1 year	671	36	855	35
1 - 2 years	366	18	464	19
2 - 3 years	242	13	318	13
3 - 4 years	186	10	244	10
4 - 5 years	75	4	122	5
5 - 10 years	205	11	244	10
Over 10 years	149	8	196	8

Length of Service in London Households by Specific Category

	General Servants	Cooks	Housemaids	Others
Servants who at time of survey had been in same household for	%	%	%	%
Under 1 year	47	33	35	34
1 - 2 years	16	18	21	18
2 - 3 years	12	13	15	13
3 - 4 years	8	10	10	10
4 - 5 years	3	4	5	3
5 - 10 years	9	13	8	12
Over 10 years	5	9	6	10

Source: C. Collet, 'Money Wages of In-Door Domestic Servants',
Parliamentary Papers, 1899, XCII, pp.25-26.

hiring a stranger. Servants on their part appealed to their acquaintances in service when seeking a new position. The informal network of natives from a particular area of the countryside probably played a very significant role in the placement of new migrants to the cities. The clustering of natives of the same locality in a single apartment house or one city block suggests that this network was more extensive and more important in placing urban domestics than the established agencies and philanthropic organisations. Placement through personal contacts was a much older and a generally less painful way of finding a domestic position.

During the nineteenth century, however, agencies became an important aspect of servant life when the enormous increase in urban migrants and the frequency of job-changing necessitated some kind of intermediary. Most servants probably had recourse to an agency or registry of some kind after 1850. The Metropolitan Association for Befriending Young Servants was founded in London in 1875. Its function at first was largely to carry on the work of the Poor Laws in placing poor women and children in domestic positions,[40] but the registry offices of the M.A.B.Y.S. handled thousands of requests from young women for positions after 1880. Throughout the 1880s, about 7,000 girls per year applied for places through M.A.B.Y.S., and of these about 5,000 per year were placed.[41] The Girls' Friendly Society also had registration offices throughout London and tried to create a system of contacts for servants who were coming to London from the countryside or who were moving about within London, so that a member of the Society need never have to feel that she was without friends in a strange place.[42] Since there were over 240,000 female domestics in London in 1881, however, the registry offices obviously dealt with only a small percentage of the job-seekers. In the early twentieth century, the Women's Employment Bureau provided a publicly-subsidised placement service but in the years between 1909 and 1913, the Bureau succeeded in placing fewer than one-fifth of the women who applied for domestic positions.[43] Obviously, most servants could not depend simply on placement services for jobs, even though they increasingly made use of such services.

As in England, the French government had long been involved in the placement of domestic servants as part of the solution to the problem of poverty. In addition, a royal administration had set up a series of offices in the seventeenth century to secure wet nurses for Parisian infants.[44] In the nineteenth century, governmental agencies continued to place orphans, abandoned children, and rehabilitated juvenile delinquents as domestics but gradually expanded their involvement in the placement of servants. Meanwhile, a variety of private agencies were instituted for this purpose such as the Servants of Mary, a religious order who founded a home for unemployed servants in Paris,[45] or the Ladies of Providence, who trained orphans for service.[46] In 1852, Louis Napoleon attempted to create a government monopoly over the employment market by licensing agencies since the controls over urban unemployment 'too evidently concern the public order'.[47] By 1909, an investigation of the system revealed that there were 203 authorised agencies which exclusively placed servants in Paris.[48]

The regulation of French agencies meant that by 1890 most servants had some contact with the placement machinery. Between 1893 and

1897, agencies of all kinds throughout France reported an average of 999,389 requests for placement per year.[49] The number of job offers they received was smaller – 716,344 per year. The total number of placements effected by agencies annually was only 349,520, or about 35 per cent of the total number of requests and less than half the number of places offered. Clearly, the agencies were not very effective in placing the large number of servants whom they were so willing to register. Nevertheless, the total number of placements by agencies in the 1890s reflects a very significant percentage of servants. The level of placements actually accomplished corresponded to approximately 38 per cent of the total number of servants (916,970 in 1896). Unless the employment agencies were dealing only with a very small group which changed jobs very often, they were handling much of the hiring which occurred after 1890. Their activities suggest a high rate of job-changing and entry into service, but this is almost certainly a decline from the peak period of the growth of the servant class before 1880. The labour market was changing at the end of the nineteenth century and the agencies themselves played an important role in this change.

French regulation of the agencies had also, by the 1890s, brought the French system closer to the placement system of England, although it did not completely eliminate the problems of the agencies nor totally assuage servants' and employers' fears of being cheated. There were basically three complaints about hiring practices in general and about the registries in particular in the nineteenth century. The first related to the supply of domestic labour *vis-à-vis* the number of jobs available. The second concerned the cost of the fees and commissions charged by the registries to servants. The third involved complaints of outright fraud.

Notwithstanding the low rates of unemployment among servants, the activities of agencies and recruiters could unquestionably encourage excessive migration to the cities by prospective domestic servants. In some cases, the agencies may have facilitated the transition to urban life, especially when the servant was assured of a position. In other cases, however, the agencies exacerbated the confusion and hardship of the urban servant who was out of work. Agencies competed with each other to win the job offers from employers and to register the largest numbers of servants. The French agencies did not share information, unlike the registry offices of the M.A.B.Y.S. of London; thus, even when there were positions available in Paris, the servant might not have access to them through a given agency. Moreover, French servants had to pay a fee for registering at an agency, and the fee could range as high as 2 francs,[50] the equivalent of an average day's wage for a female worker, and had to be paid without any guarantee of placement. After placement, the servant owed the agency a percentage of the first month's or first year's wage.[51] The arithmetic in this system clearly worked to the servant's disadvantage. The fee was due when the servant began to work so that if the position were short-lived, the domestic might end up paying nearly all of the first month's wages for a job that lasted only that long. Octave Mirbeau's heroine Celestine took seven places in four and a half months and had to pay an agency 3 per cent of seven years' wages plus the registration fee.[52] The cost of placement was transferred entirely to the French employer by legislation in 1904 but until then the agencies could hamper the job search more than they helped.

Even more damaging to the reputation of placement agencies in France were the charges of outright fraud, including the suspicion that some agents acted as recruiters for houses of prostitution.[53] Although it is impossible to judge how frequently agents lured young women into prostitution rather than directing them to legitimate domestic positions, these charges were not simply rumour. In 1912, a complaint by a young female chambermaid in Paris led to an investigation which revealed the fact that the house in which she, two other chambermaids, one laundress, one governess and one cook worked was in fact a brothel.[54] The young chambermaid had been sent to the house two weeks before in answer to her request for a domestic position. And an official investigation by the French Commission on Work in 1895 concluded that there were far too many cases in which a servant was sent to a false address or to a place where a servant had already been hired.[55] As a result of such frauds, both servants and employers were reluctant to deal with agents.

In England, the most common means of securing a servant other than through personal contacts was to advertise in the newspapers. This method, at a minor cost to the employer, allowed English employers to circumvent the problem of dealing through agencies and meant that a vacant position was more widely known among unemployed domestics. Servant-subscribed journals tried to play an increasing role in publicising domestic vacancies but none of them lasted more than a few months.[56] Although there was much discussion of the importance of servants' own organisations, these associations played a very minor role in the domestic employment market.

French servants' associations began in the 1880s to emulate the English in publishing job advertisements and servants' requests for positions. More successful than the English servant newspapers, two French servants' journals lasted seven and twenty-three years respectively.[57] The English servant newspapers had to compete with numerous middle-class women's journals, whereas the French publications had virtually no competition.[58] But even by the beginning of the twentieth century in France, the servants' own associations were not very important in helping servants to find positions.[59]

By the 1880s, in other words, France was experiencing a significant change in some of the characteristics of urban domestic service. In

England, the transition was not so clearly marked nor did it necessarily coincide chronologically with the French development. In France, while somewhat more servants were beginning to view the occupation as permanent and as the servant population was ageing, the job market was tightening up and coming under the growing control of agencies. The fact that jobs were growing harder to find made the agencies more important. In this way, the evolution of more restrictive machinery for hiring dovetailed with the declining demand for servants.

The English transition was different in character and perhaps in timing. Because of misleading census categories, precise dating of the decline of servants in England is impossible. It appears that the decline occurred in England about the same time as in France. But the decline in England was not accompanied and reinforced by the tightening up of the job market. In the first place, the unskilled labour supply in England had long been more plentiful than in France, at least in terms of accessibility to the cities.[60] Second, the customary methods of hiring were different in England; personal contacts or newspaper advertisement had consistently accounted for much more of the hiring than agencies or organisations of whatever kind. In addition to the greater supply of unskilled labour, England, a more heavily urbanised country, had less need of the organisations which facilitated the long-range migration of French domestics. A greater proportion of English servants were drawn from the cities themselves or from the immediately-surrounding suburbs, so that they could more easily secure positions through personal contacts or through newspaper advertisements.[61] Nevertheless, in England as in France, the number of domestic positions was declining because many middle-class budgets could no longer sustain the employment of servants. Unemployment among English servants seems to have been increasing[62] and, because of their plentiful supply, English servants at the end of the nineteenth century were suffering greater hardships through unemployment than their French counterparts.

Placement was in fact, like domestic service itself, a two-edged sword. Difficulties in finding a job could greatly heighten the difficulties of adjusting to urban life which a new immigrant faced, particularly if lured by exaggerated promises from an agency. Some servants found themselves downwardly mobile and suffered total anomie.[63] Even placement through personal contacts did not insure an easy transition. The degree to which relatives or natives of the same area of France, acting as extended kin, may have eased the transition to the city of other migrants remains problematical.[64] But the placement figures at the end of the century reveal that many servants found new jobs and that many of these jobs proved reasonably secure. When the network of agencies, recruiters, and informal contacts facilitated the acculturation process, then these servants enjoyed a secure foundation in the cities from which a certain degree of social mobility could be expected. Thus, an assessment of placement suggests that the more important question is an evaluation of servants, occupational and social mobility in the nineteenth century.

5. SOCIAL MOBILITY

'Thus, at sixteen, I entered into a career of drudgery where long hours, low wages and very often inadequate food were accepted standards of a life that was thrust on one out of sheer necessity,' begins the autobiography of Lavinia Swainbank, an English housemaid.[1] Why this life of considerable hardship and not-infrequent mistreatment should have continued to attract so many people into the ranks of servants, even after industrialisation provided alternative employment for some, is an important and recurring question in the study of nineteenth-century domestic service. Lavinia Swainbank and others like her felt they had no other options. But for many others who had an alternative to servanthood, the answer lies elsewhere. Many servants clearly felt well compensated for their drudgery, as we discussed in a previous chapter. Another aspect of the explanation was the traditional character of domestic service for rural, and particularly female, labour. In other words, traditional socialisation encouraged young female peasants to enter service, but so did the attractive wages and other benefits. But any explanation must involve an additional crucial factor — the possibility of social mobility through service.

Servants' aspirations most often reflected traditional, family-centred goals and their motivation for entering service was the support which they could provide for their families. Many servants left bequests at their deaths to surviving relatives whom they had left behind in the countryside,[2] which suggests a continuing contact with the rural milieu from which most servants came. Some servants returned to their natal villages to retire on their savings.[3] During their lives in service, servants often helped to support their families in the countryside. This tradition was particularly strong in France, where smallholding agriculture declined much more slowly than in England, because this contribution was often necessary to the maintenance of the family land. An example of this practice is found in the papers of the Flauhaut family in the Pas-de-Calais covering the first half of the nineteenth century. The records of this cultivator note the percentage deducted from the annual wages of servants to be sent to the servant's family; the average percentage deducted was 20 per cent.[4] In England, this practice persisted mainly among the Irish and Welsh who worked in England as servants since these immigrants usually came from tenant-farmer backgrounds.[5] Rowntree noted for the city of York that he found little evidence of this practice among servants who came from York itself.[6] The practice also served to provide for aged parents for whom single servants were supposed to feel a special responsibility.[7] This need to provide assistance to one's family supplied an important motivation for a servant's entry into domestic work rather than some other kind of job and helped to shape a servant's aspirations. But gradually other, more personal goals also shaped the patterns of servant mobility.

There were cases in the nineteenth century of servants who experienced sudden and dramatic upward mobility by inheriting a fortune at the death of a grateful employer or by marrying into the family of an employer, but the evidence not surprisingly suggests that this involved only a very small minority. Upwardly mobile servants commonly advanced in social status much more gradually and to a more limited degree. Marriage was the most important means for a female servant to be mobile since most women married in the nineteenth century and their status was then defined by the occupation of their spouses. Male servants could also marry upward by selecting younger mates in imitation of the new middle-class pattern or by marrying older women with considerable savings or some property, but they used marriage as a mobility channel less often than their female counterparts.

Occupational mobility provided another significant channel for social mobility. Throughout the nineteenth century, upwardly mobile servants used the period of service to acquire either the skills or the working capital or both to launch a small commercial venture or to buy some property. Overall, domestic servants experienced a considerable amount of mobility, upward, downward and lateral.

Service was, in sociological terms, a 'bridging occupation', that is, an occupation which provides the conditions and opportunities which facilitate the movement from one occupation to another.[8] In the case of male servants, the function of domestic service as a bridge to other occupations was more important than its role as an apprenticeship for marriage, which is doubtless why male servants could marry more freely, in accordance with newer kinds of personal tastes. In the first place, men's experiences as servants better prepared them for skilled occupations. The overwhelming majority of male servants worked in households which employed more than two servants: thus, male servants performed more specialised tasks and assumed greater responsibility than most female servants for household management. Within an extensive domestic hierarchy, male servants were invariably at the top, and their opportunities for mobility within the hierarchy were greater than those for women. Moreover, the commercialised sectors of personal service were more often filled by males so that male servants had more extensive occupational opportunities even in the service sector: for example, a groom might become a public coachman; a cook, a hotel chef; a valet, a secretary. Women servants also experienced internal mobility by acquiring cooking or management skills with which they could gain positions as cooks or housekeepers, but their occupational opportunities outside of service were more limited than those of men.

But the fact is that, as in most non-agricultural occupations, female servants usually quit their jobs after a few years, most of them to marry and not to return to formal employment in their previous job area. Marriage ended their period of formal employment although many continued to work intermittently to supplement the family income. The woman's occupation before marriage could, however, be relevant to her marriage. In the cases of mobility via marriage, service had a number of advantages, and we must assume that many young women endured the job because of their ambitions for their future. As a base for conventional mobility, service allowed the accumulation of savings, acquisition of certain crucial traits, like literacy or even personal grooming habits, and established access to information about other occupations. Some women would take advantage of this throughout the century.

The most important factors in the preparation of the servant for mobility either through occupational changes or through marriage were the exposure to basic education, delay of marriage, and the opportunity to save nearly the entire wage toward a future marriage or career or property investment. And although most servants did not remain in service after marriage, family limitation by married couples in service was a fourth factor in upward mobility; the slightly later marriage age was due partially to the structure of servanthood but also partially by design, and ex-servants had fewer children than the urban lower classes in general. A fifth, much more speculative factor might be included — that part of the motivation for entering domestic service was a desire for upward mobility — thus this desire to escape agricultural poverty could be translated into the will to succeed. Such aspirations, whatever their original source, were undoubtedly enhanced by the contact with middle-class values, since the middle classes, by and large, are more achievement-oriented than the lower classes.[9] The middle classes often proselytised among the servant class for their values of family limitation, encouragement of their children's achievement, saving for the future and personal self-discipline, in contrast to the lower-class focus on immediate rewards. However effective the middle-class moralisation campaign overall, the servants' interaction with the middle class must have communicated to some servants the middle-class aspirations for upward mobility.

One of the most important factors in occupational mobility was education. In a middle- or upper-class household, the servant was often exposed to the rudiments of education. Lamartine's novel, *Geneviève*, was dedicated to his family's servant who had been taught to read and write with the daughters of the family.[10] Employers had to educate their own servants, because servants received no formal training for their occupation. A constant theme of reformers in the nineteenth century was the need for the formal education of domestics,[11] but as we have seen, attempts before 1900 to institute professional domestic training were a failure.[12] By the turn of the twentieth century, primary school education was just beginning to have an effect on rural illiteracy, so that nineteenth-century employers could expect their new servants to be illiterate and often crude. Even by 1920, English girls continued to leave school at thirteen or fourteen, having learned little more than some reading and writing.[13] The humble backgrounds of most servants did not prepare them with the 'genteel accomplishments'. Employers trained their own servants because of the lag in the educational system, and this personal training, if haphazard, was far more important than the general training schemes — perhaps more than ordinary schooling until the early 1900s.

The education which servants received at the hands of their employers had two ends — to moralise them and to increase their usefulness as servants. Hence, the content of this training included little more than very practical instruction in domestic skills, some attempts at moral and hygienic lessons, basic arithmetic and some inspirational reading. There was often some free time in the afternoons or evenings when employers would try to keep servants busy by putting them to work at improving their handwriting or practising their arithmetic.[14] Many of the handbooks on domestic service were written for servants' self-improvement; and though perhaps pandering to middle-class expectations more than realities, at the very least these manuals imply a high level of literacy among servants even at mid-century.

For those who chose to be informed by the literature aimed at them, domestic service was always considered to be a good feminine occupation because 'it is good training for married life'.[15] Through reading, female servants were supposed to 'learn habits of personal cleanliness and neatness, punctuality, obedience, good manners, and general discipline,'[16] so that the 'working class man then finds his home more clean, neat, comfortable, and his meals more palatable yet economical.'[17] Because of the nature of domestic service, servants came into the occupation unskilled — 'almost anyone can be a servant'[18] — but often had the opportunity to develop skills which facilitated mobility, and reading as well as direct experience had its role to play here.

Although literacy statistics are very difficult to find for the nineteenth century, it is clear from the few available data that servants were more literate than other lower-class individuals of rural origins. In Lyons at the end of the eighteenth century, 58 per cent of the male servants and 33 per cent of the female servants could sign their acts of marriage.[19] Though the ability to sign one's name is a weak test of literacy, this index alone distinguished the servant class from the rest of the lower classes whose literacy level was still lower. In Lyons in 1872 this high level of literacy continued to characterise the servant class. In a sampling of Lyons' servants, 78.3 per cent of the female servants could read and write, and 13 per cent more could read; only 8.7 per cent could neither read nor write.[20] This level of literacy was considerably higher than that of the populations of the areas from which most of them came.[21] By 1901, French government statistics point out the servant class as a uniquely literate group among the lower classes. Male servants were 89 per cent literate in 1901 and female servants were 85 per cent literate.[22] This high rate of literacy is most striking when compared to the illiteracy of the agricultural population from which most servants were drawn: of the total population, only 73 per cent were literate.[23] Clearly, most servants were better prepared for social mobility in this regard than other rural-born lower-class people.

Literacy was an essential element in the servant's complete adaptation to the urban milieu. The basic skills of reading and writing were important prerequisites for the clerical and commercial occupations which represented occupational mobility for some servants. Literacy was also a valuable asset to a female servant who married a shopkeeper or artisan, and who could thereby help out in the family business. Thus, servants' high level of literacy defined them

Table 5.1 Civil status of servants

A: Versailles, 1836

| | Servants | | Total Population | |
	% Males	% Females	% Males	% Females
Single	61.6	78.8	50.2	48.5
Married	32.8	11.9	44.9	35.5
Widowed	5.6	9.3	4.9	16.0

B: London, 1851

| | Servants | | Total Population |
	% Males	% Females	% Females
Single	77.0	93.4	76.0
Married	19.9	2.0)	
Widowed	3.1	4.6)	24.0

C: France, 1901

| | Servants | | Total Population | |
	% Males	% Females	% Males	% Females
Single	39.6	65.4	52.7	47.0
Married	56.0	21.3	41.9	40.7
Widowed	4.3	13.3	5.3	12.3

Source: A: Versailles, Listes nominatives, 1836; B: *Census of England and Wales,* 1851, manuscript census lists; C: *Statistique générale,* 1901, IV, 511.

as a group particularly disposed to upward mobility.

Female servants' mobility was most clearly evident in their marriage patterns, that is, both when they married and in what circumstances. Delayed marriage was an almost inevitable condition of domestic service, but it also constituted a strong advantage in upward mobility. Live-in domestics usually did not marry and remain in service, although male servants were more likely to do so than female domestics (Table 5.1). Female urban migrants particularly used service as an interim occupation before marriage, so that they could accumulate dowries and establish themselves in the city, and this often paid off in marriages to spouses of somewhat higher social status.

The marrying ages of servants demonstrate a striking pattern of delayed marriage (Tables 5.2, 5.3 and 5.4). Most servants clearly married very late; 42 per cent of Bordeaux's female servants and 45 per cent of those in Versailles married at the age of 30 or older (Table 5.4). Male servants married even later. And the contrast between the ages of male and female servants and their non-servant spouses indicates some interesting conclusions. First, the male servants were marrying women considerably younger than they. Seventy-two per cent of the non-servant wives were under 30 and 50 per cent were under 25 (Table 5.3). Thus, male servants were marrying younger women in imitation of a middle-class pattern, apparently unconcerned about securing the more substantial dowries that older women were more likely to provide. But more important is the fact that female servants were doing the opposite. Women domestics were marrying late and their spouses also tended to be rather older than the general average. Moreover, out of the 692 marriages in this category, 105 of the non-servant spouses had been married before, whereas only 12 of the servants had been. While this suggests that older female servants may have had greater difficulty in finding husbands since the men with whom they worked tended to marry younger women, it is at least as significant that older men were also more likely to be men of some property.

Table 5.2 Servants' age at marriage, comparing Versailles and Bordeaux

| | Bordeaux in 1872 | | Versailles, 1825-1853 | |
	% Males	% Females	% Males	% Females
Under 19	1.5	2.2	0.4	2.9
20 - 24	11.1	22.7	16.4	18.4
25 - 29	33.3	31.2	37.1	33.6
30 - 34	26.9	22.7	31.9	24.1
35 - 39	14.2	13.5	7.3	10.7
40 - 44	7.9	4.1	4.7	4.9
45 -	4.5	2.3	2.5	5.5

Source: For Bordeaux, Jarlin, p.40; for Versailles, Série E, Actes de Mariage et Contrats de Mariage, 1825-1853.

English servants, on the other hand, married at an age closer to the average for working women (Table 5.4). They spent somewhat less time in service than French servants on the whole, though they often began service earlier. Even so, despite an undeniable contrast which reflects the fuller urbanisation of English servants, they too, like their French counterparts, were older than most women when they married — a delay for which the experience of domestic service must have accounted. In other words, despite the absence of a neat servant marriage pattern, something of a generalisation does emerge. Most servants married and ended their formal employment when they married. They married later than the norm, though this pattern was more decisive in France because of its propertied agricultural traditions and the greater importance of formal dowries.[24] Later marriage improved their chances of marrying better, and this was true in highly urbanised London just as in the slower-paced, traditional society of Bordeaux.

Servants complained that marriage disqualified them for positions as live-in domestics, and it is true that employers were reluctant to employ married servants because it involved too many problems and a conflict of interests.[25] Only when barring a servant's marriage threatened the servant's morals was the employer in theory willing for the servant to marry,[26] and in fact many preferred simply to seek a replacement. If a female servant remained in service after marriage, she sometimes had to live separated from her husband. Male servants' housing was governed by more flexible arrangements so that a male domestic could generally be separately housed while fulfilling the duties of a live-in domestic. There were also some cases of couples in service together. In the sample of London households in 1851, there were only three cases of couples in service together: ranging in age from mid-thirties to mid-forties, none of the couples had children living with them. But the whole point is this: whatever their ambition, many female servants were pressed into a later-than-average marriage age by the stark knowledge that they had to choose between job and wedlock.

As a result of the obstacles to marriage and because of the transitional nature of domestic service, very few servants married and remained in service. But it is difficult to pin down the precise percentage of servants who never married since many left service for other occupations or moved in and out of the occupation at different periods. However, it is likely that servants who reached the age of 45 without marrying would never marry and this group was rather small. In Lyons in 1872, 9 per cent of the female servants and 12 per cent of the males were unmarried at the age of 45 or older.[27] In the London sample from 1851 and 1871, only 4·6 per cent of the female servants and 2·3 per cent of the males remained unmarried at 45. It is clear, then, that the overwhelming majority of servants were single (Table 5.1), and that most left service at a relatively young age, either to marry or to change occupations. And this suggests the more important point. There may have been agonies

Table 5.3. Servants' age at marriage, Versailles, 1825-1833, 1845-1853

Age at marriage	Two Servant Marriages		One Servant Marriages			
	% Males	% Females	% Male Servant	% Wife	% Husband	% Female Servant
15 - 19	–	3.0	1.5	12.3	1.2	2.9
20 - 24	14.3	21.4	21.5	38.5	16.9	17.6
25 - 29	40.5	35.1	27.7	21.5	31.4	33.2
30 - 34	32.1	28.6	30.8	13.8	20.1	23.0
35 - 39	7.1	7.7	7.7	6.2	11.0	11.4
40 - 44	4.2	1.2	6.2	6.2	5.8	5.8
45 - 49	1.2	1.8	3.1	1.5	4.9	3.6
50 - 54	0.6	0.6	–	–	3.0	1.4
55 - 59	–	0.6	–	–	2.5	0.9
60 - 64	–	–	1.5	–	1.9	0.1
65 -	–	–	–	–	1.4	–
Number of cases	168		65		692	

over the choice between job and mate; there were practical difficulties in meeting eligible males. But surely part of the servants' marriage pattern resulted from an accident such as the death of a local shopkeeper's spouse, that made one of their daily male contacts eligible and themselves desirable, for servants did not intend to let the job interfere with broader concerns.

Young women found servanthood a useful and respectable occupation before marriage and it enabled them to save money which could be used to provide a dowry when they married. Servants, when they married, often were able to make 'good' marriages, that is to men of the urban shopkeeping or artisanal classes. Although based upon limited French data on servant marriages, the pattern of these marriages is clear. What the interpretation of the data should be is not so obvious, but there are two models which are effective in indicating what was happening. First, servant marriages can be viewed in terms of the fusing of occupational or social categories from the rural milieu to those of the city through the marriage of rural-born individuals to urban residents. In this model, marriage becomes a measure of the social endogamy being created by the massive urban migrations of the nineteenth century. Second, servant marriages can be seen against some kind of social ladder which servants climbed by marrying men of lower or higher occupational statuses. Here, marriage is used to measure degrees of upward and downward social mobility.

The key point in both models is that marriage meant for most servants the end of a transitional period — the end of service and a settling down in the urban environment — and it frequently represented an improvement in their social status. As Fig. 5.1 indicates, these servants were clearly moving from agricultural backgrounds into the urban milieu of the artisanal and shopkeeping classes. Hence, service was a crucial link between the traditional, agricultural societies from which most servants came and the modern urban societies which they were helping to create.[28] In itself, service was merely a channel for this mobility, albeit an important one. This may be all that we could or should say about the effect of domestic service in the period of industrialisation. But the second model, which emphasises the marriage patterns of a significant minority of servants (Table 5.5), suggests something more. The second model indicates that service was not simply a neutral channel for urban migration but that the experience of domestic service was itself a contributing factor in urban acculturation. This model implies that servants were better off than other urban migrants because of the unique experiences offered by their jobs.

Without a comprehensive study of occupational and social mobility in the industrial period, it is difficult to evaluate degrees of social mobility for any particular group accurately and, above all, for females in any social class. Moreover, the second model suggests a perhaps too highly stratified and too static conception of social status. But by

Table 5.4 Age at marriage of English servants in 1901

Age of Marriage	Female Servants %	1000 Working Women %	Age of Marriage	Female Servants %	1000 Working Women %
Under 18	3.4	1.2	24	16.3	10.5
18	0.6	2.4	25	11.8	8.8
19	3.4	9.7	26	3.9	3.1
20	5.6	13.0	27	—	0.7
21	18.5	16.3	28	2.3	1.2
22	14.0	13.8	29	1.1	0.4
23	16.3	17.2	30	1.7	0.5
			Over 30	1.1	1.2

comparing the occupations of female servants' parents with those of their spouses, it is possible to infer that from one-quarter to one-third of servants upon marrying bettered their social status. It is clear, for example, that twice as many servants married artisans and shopkeepers than came from artisanal and shopkeeping backgrounds.

The study of the marriage records of French servants unmistakably reveals that some servants remained in service until they were financially secure enough to marry well. Of the servants who married in Versailles between 1825 and 1853 and whose marriages were covered by contracts (155 cases), only three declared no property at all at the time of their marriages.[29] Most of the cases demonstrated that servants had accumulated substantial savings; the majority had at least 1,000 francs, about three to four years' wages for a female servant in this period (Table 5.6). Female domestics often brought as much or more property to the marriage as did their spouses even though their prospective husbands were in commercial or skilled occupations. The conclusion is that better preparation for marriage through delaying marrying and accumulating savings resulted in the servants improving their social position, however slightly, through marriage.

As Table 5.5 demonstrates, the general trend was similar in Versailles between 1825 and 1853 and in Bordeaux in 1872, but the two patterns also reveal some important differences. There was an even greater movement of female servants into the shopkeeping and artisanal classes in Bordeaux. The differences point to the more balanced economy of Bordeaux, a port town with a large commercial class. Versailles, much smaller and probably higher in *per capita* income, was a fashionable suburb of Paris with a numerous upper class who employed more servants per household than were employed in Bordeaux. The pattern of marriage for Bordeaux's servants was, thus, more indicative of the national pattern for the traditional cities outside the Parisian orbit.

Consequently, using the second model for servant marriage patterns, the servants experiencing upward social mobility through marriage constituted about one-third of the total. The upwardly mobile were clearly more numerous than those who made contracts (about one in six); hence, it is probable that many marriages which involved some property were not covered by contract and/or that in some cases the relevant skills which the spouses possessed were more important than property. The significant factor was that servants' spouses in one-third of the cases can be occupationally classified as belonging to a rather higher social level.

Though we have no similar data on English servants, some conclusions can be suggested on the basis of qualitative evidence. First of all, as already noted, the formal dowry was more important in France than in England and the delay of marriage was consequently more pronounced among the French than among the English. But English servants, like the French, often deliberately entered service with the intention of

92

Fig. 5.1. Occupational comparison of servants' parents and spouses

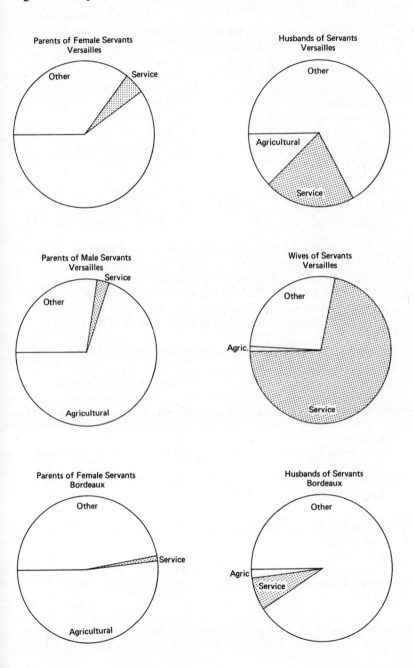

Parents of Female Servants
Versailles

Other   Service

Husbands of Servants
Versailles

Other

Agricultural

Service

Parents of Male Servants
Versailles

Other   Service

Agricultural

Wives of Servants
Versailles

Other

Agric.

Service

Parents of Female Servants
Bordeaux

Other

Service

Agricultural

Husbands of Servants
Bordeaux

Other

Agric   Service

Table 5.5. Servants' Parents and Spouses, Versailles and Bordeaux

| | Versailles Occupational Classification of Female Servants' | | Bordeaux | |
	Parents %	Spouses %	Parents %	Spouses %
Agriculture	57·7	12·6	52·8	4·0
Shopkeeping, managerial	04·3	8·4	7·6	20·6
Public sector	1·4	8·5	0·8	4·3
Working class	19·5	21·5	7·6	25·5
Artisanal	8·1	17·4	4·8	17·0
Employee	2·6	4·9	0·8	13·5
Domestic service, services	3·8	22·6	1·2	11·3
Other, No Profession	2·6	4·2	24·1	3·8

Source: Versailles — Archives départementales, Série É, Actes de Mariages et Contrats de Mariage, 1825-1853; Bordeaux — Françoise Jarlin, *Les Domestiques à Bordeaux en 1872* (Bordeaux: University of Bordeaux, T.E.R., 1969), p.40 ff.

Table 5.6. Servants' wealth at marriage, Versailles, 1825-1853

| | Marriages of Female Servants | |
1825-33 francs	Husband %	Servant %
Under 499	40·1	3·0
500 - 1,999	27·8	29·6
2,000 - 3,999	14·8	31·5
4,000 - 9,999	9·3	22·3
10,000 -	7·5	3·6
1845-53		
Under 499 fr.	32·9	8·6
500 - 1,999	31·4	35·7
2,000 - 3,999	14·3	34·3
4,000 - 9,999	11·4	17·2
10,000 -	2·8	1·4

marrying well.[30] Their chief contacts, like their French sisters, were with other servants, soldiers and sailors, or the shopkeepers and artisans who supplied their employers' households. While the lesser importance of the dowry in England suggests that the English domestic was less likely to profit from a period in service to accumulate a dowry, other factors such as family size and consumption patterns indicate that English servants too had high personal aspirations.

Servants' later marriage age in both France and England was also a natural limit to family size. Servants in the nineteenth century maintained one of the smallest average family sizes of any occupational group; in France in 1911, servants' average number of children was 1·6, compared with 2 for industrial workers and 2·25 for agricultural workers.[31] Of the servants who listed children in 1872 in Lyons, 50 per cent of them had only one child.[32] In Versailles in that year, 83 per cent of the servant couples had only one child.[33] In the London sample of 1851, none of the servant couples listed children, although generalisation is risky since the probability of married servants turning up in the sample was very small.[34] In the London sample from 1871, one servant couple listed three children.[35]

The patterns of late marriage and family limitation might indicate no more than the result of circumstances which circumscribed servants' options,[36] if it were not for indications that these patterns reflected more general attitudes, whether originating in servants' own aspirations or in the adoption of middle-class values. Servants seem to have maintained a life-style which emulated the middle classes in important respects, of which consumption is a significant example. Since servants' purchases were very limited because food and lodging were provided by their employers, one of the few items on which they could spend money was clothing. Most servants, it seems, spent a considerable amount in outfitting themselves, so much so that their contemporaries were disturbed by servants' attempts to dress like their employers.[37]

It may seem rather obvious that where servants wore livery or uniforms, they were anxious to shed those badges of servitude when they had time off, but the point suggests a host of possibilities with regard to outlook. Some servants enjoyed their uniforms — particularly the young domestic newly arrived in the city and unaccustomed to anything other than hand-me-downs. Jean Rennie, a kitchenmaid at the turn of the twentieth century, recalled years later the pleasure of 'the real feel of a black frock, a little white apron, and a white muslin cap, with black stockings and shoes.'[38] But most servants who were dressed neatly but by no means prettily at work could afford to be fancy on a Sunday outing or an occasional evening out. And especially by the beginning of the twentieth century, when many of their counterparts were part of the new white-collar class of shop assistants and business clerks, servants were conscious of wanting to dress well. As William Lanceley, a house steward, expressed it, servants needed to dress up in order to meet their friends and kin 'on something like the same footing'.[39] Rather than an act of defiance against disapproving

Table 5.7. Servants' wealth at death, Paris, 1825, 1853, 1869

	1825		1853		1869	
Francs	Males %	Females %	Males %	Females %	Males %	Females %
Under 100	8·0	30·0	5·6	4·7	–	7·1
00-499	60·0	33·3	2·8	25·6	33·3	17·9
500-999	4·0	10·0	5·6	14·0	6·7	12·5
1,000-1,999	12·0	–	16·7	32·6	6·7	17·9
2,000-3,999	4·0	20·0	16·7	11·6	–	10·7
4,000-5,999	4·0	6·7	5·6	4·7	13·3	12·5
6,000-7,999	4·0	–	5·6	4·7	–	7·1
8,000-9,999	–	–	–	–	13·3	7·1
10,000-	4·0	–	16·7	2·3	26·7	7·1
Number of cases	25	30	18	43	15	56

Source: Paris, A.D. de Paris, D. Q. 7 3417-3939 (1825), 3532-4022 (1853), 10.611-10.704 (1869), Déclarations des Mutations par décès.

mistresses, this was in fact part of a general lower-class interest in better dress as a mark of urban status. Servants' dress could well relate to a desire to gain greater respectability in other matters.

A more important aspect of servants' consumption pattern concerned their interest in saving money. Savings banks in the nineteenth century depended to a great extent on servant depositors since the working classes rarely had a surplus to put aside and were slow to use savings banks. Until mid-century at least, servants constituted by far the greatest group of depositors.[40] This habit of saving was entirely consistent both with traditional aspirations, such as sending one's wages back to one's parents, but also with servants' delay of marriage and imitation of middle-class manners and dress.

Whatever the source of servants' spending habits, the money which they put aside — and perhaps their more attractive clothes as well — could make the difference in making an advantageous marriage for a female servant or starting a new career for a male or female servant. As for the unmarried, the declarations of property at death of Parisian servants indicate that relatively few servants died literally penniless.[41] Of servants who died in Paris in 1825, 1853 and 1869, many declared considerable property (Table 5.7). Property of 1,000 francs or more would have been sufficient to duplicate a servant's previous income over a long retirement period. Even the declarations below 1,000 francs most often included some savings and/or income from investments such as railroad bonds, in addition to purely personal property. A similar study of Bordeaux in 1899 reinforces the conclusion that servants were willing and able to accumulate considerable savings (Table 5.8).

Table 5.8. Servants' wealth at death in Bordeaux, 1899 (Both Male and Female Servants)

Francs	%
50 - 1,000	33·3
1,000 - 5,000	36·7
5,000 - 10,000	16.7
10,000 - 28,500	13.3
Number of cases	30

Source: Jarlin, pp.73-75.

A period in domestic service provided rural-born individuals with an opportunity to support their parents in a very traditional way; or to prepare for a personal future in marriage or a skilled occupation, or in a minority of cases to assure their future retirement. This was part of the attraction which domestic service exercised on young peasants or the daughters of artisans and workers.[42] The initial step by which these individuals broke out of the cycle of poverty was a decision to migrate to the city, a move often of considerable distance. This initial decision signalled that many servants were more venturesome than others who remained in the countryside or sought employment nearer at hand, although the decision was obviously influenced by a long agricultural tradition. Once in domestic service, the servants' aspirations and traditional motivations came into contact with middle-class values and were shaped toward new goals for personal mobility.

Overall, in quantitative terms, about one-third of the servant group was upwardly mobile. Another third found in service either a permanent occupation or the means to accumulate enough money to return to the countryside to marry or to return to the milieu from which they had come, or to marry laterally into the urban working classes. And perhaps another third remained in the cities but were downwardly mobile. Some servants suffered severely from the hardships which service imposed and were unable to cope with its degradations, as will be examined in the succeeding chapter. Nevertheless, the experience of service was the experience of a transitional period in an individual's life, as it was in the modernisation of the society more generally. Thus, although servants' fates after leaving service were diverse and difficult to pin down, what became of them upon leaving service is probably more important than service itself.

6. DEFIANCE AND DOWNWARD MOBILITY

Whatever advantages domestic service offered to urban immigrants in the nineteenth century, the occupation remained associated with the unpleasant aspects of middle-class existence — with the dirt and the garbage of urban life. Moreover, an integral part of live-in domestic service had always been the debasing experience of inferiority. Coping with that experience need not have been troublesome. Lavinia Swainbank recalls the attempt to turn her into 'a well-oiled machine' as 'splendid basic training'.[1] Many servants, as noted in the previous chapter, obviously drew considerable profit from the experience of servitude, for even the servant who internalised the feelings of inferiority might emerge from service determined that her children would have a better life. Other servants became defiant in the face of employer snobbery, as we shall see. Still others could not or would not adapt to their situation in middle-class households in the cities and were unable to make a successful transition from domestic service to other occupations or to marriage.

Employers in the nineteenth century felt deeply threatened by servants who refused to be deferent. They ascribed servants' defiance to dishonesty, sexual promiscuity, and even criminality. But the middle classes were not simply expressing their paranoia in these impressions. The servant population had high rates of illegitimate births, thefts, drunkenness, prostitution, infanticide, suicide. In fact, a substantial segment of the servant class was downwardly mobile and ended up among the disreputable poor. The combination of both upward and downward mobility through domestic service helps to explain the status ambiguity of the servant class and the ambivalence of attitudes toward domestic work.

Sources to document domestics' alienation from their work are much more fragmentary than those for social mobility. Much of the material is sketchy and impressionistic; the comments of observers are often unreliable and generally fail to provide quantitative evidence for their conclusions. Statistics on health and crime were rarely classified according to occupational groups in the nineteenth century. As a result, the discussion of alienation and downward mobility must be limited, unless one wishes a catalogue of spicy horror stories, although this element of service was equally as significant as the possibility for upward mobility.

Some of the causes of the servants' alienation from their work are the now familiar conditions of long hours, miserable housing, virtual loss of freedom, and an often degrading master-servant relationship.

The placement machinery also contributed to the hardships of many recent urban immigrants, and urban life itself in the nineteenth century was fraught with hazards. Special dangers for servants were the periods of unemployment, prolonged illness, old age and motherhood; all of these factors aggravated the burden of servants' normal working conditions and caused some servants to turn to 'solutions' such as alcoholism, infanticide and suicide.

Unemployment was perhaps the most serious dilemma for servants who turned to crime or prostitution when confronted with the problems of finding housing and supporting themselves in a hostile environment. Notwithstanding the relatively low official rate of unemployment and the fact that servants probably were unemployed less often than other lower-class groups, servants often suffered a dead season when employers left the cities during the summer for resorts.[2] The length of the period of unemployment among French servants in 1896 showed a definite pattern of one- and two-month lay-offs, which was probably the result of the summer dead season.[3] Some employers dismissed their servants without warning for this period, and the number of unemployed servants 'tripled or quadrupled' during the summer months.

Illness also frequently cut into a servant's career, leaving him unemployed, in a public hospital, and desperate for some means of support. Although the domestic economy manuals emphasised the responsibility of masters to care for their servants during illnesses,[4] many apparently simply dismissed their underlings if they felt they could hire another servant easily.[5] Certain diseases, notably tuberculosis, attacked provincial immigrants to the cities much more frequently than the urban-born, and servants in particular suffered disproportionately because of their inadequate housing. Syphilis was also considered to be an occupational hazard for servants, and this disease may have prematurely ended some servants' careers.[6] Finally, advancing age increased the difficulties of finding a new position for the minority of servants who did not marry, as the stagnating wages of servants after the age of thirty-five already suggested.

Increasing age was an important problem for domestic servants, even though we deal here only with the small segment that tried to stay on in the occupation, if only for lack of alternatives. Since the occupation was almost exclusively a young woman's apprenticeship for marriage, older men and women, in spite of their experience, often found themselves undesirable as live-in domestics. The high level of mobility within this occupation meant that a servant either acquired specific skills and moved into the positions like cook which demanded certain skills and experience, or was forced to take lower paid, less desirable domestic positions in order to be employed at all as she aged. Since the maid-of-all-work or general domestic was usually 'just a stepping-stone to a more trained position',[7] only the incompetents remained general servants for long. Women over forty who had either failed to move into a more skilled domestic position or who had been out of service for some time often supported themselves by day work or 'charing'. Charwomen or 'femmes de ménage' were primarily women who were untrained and who had to resort to domestic work to provide for themselves and their families when family income declined for some reason.[8] During the peak decades of servanthood, charing was a temporary solution for some married women who needed to supplement their husbands' income which had declined because of the husband's illness or temporary unemployment. Other charwomen were women who because of widowhood or desertion or inability to perform other kinds of work had to depend on whatever income they themselves could earn.[9] Charwomen were older than live-in domestics and most were married or had been married at some time: 49 per cent of English charwomen in 1911 were widows while only an additional 30 per cent were married.[10] In 1901 in England, 77 per cent of the charwomen were either married or widowed,[11] so that the proportion of single women in charing was declining at the beginning of the twentieth century even though the percentage had never been very large. Thus, charing or daily work remained a refuge for the unskilled woman, even as live-in domestic service began to decline.

Since charing was increasingly the occupation of people too old to continue other occupations, whatever their previous job background, servants who were unable to find positions because of their age had

Table 6.1. Employed active French population over 65 in 1901

	Males %	Females %
Agriculture	3·1	3·6
Industry	2·5	2·8
Commerce	1·6	1·5
Domestic Service	5·2	4·0

Source: *Statistique générale*, 1901, IV, 215.

almost no future. It is clear from the age structure of the servant population that although service was usually an occupation of the young, it also attracted a much higher percentage of people over sixty than other occupations (Table 6.1). In London in 1851, 25 per cent of the women over sixty-five who continued to work were servants. Yet despite the fact that service was one of the few employment options for the aged, contemporary sources indicate that there was considerable prejudice against hiring servants after the age of forty-five.[12] The only alternatives for a servant who aged and failed to marry, according to the British Women's Industrial Council, were, first, to invest her savings in a lodging house with a partner; second, to keep house for a relative; third, to live on her savings until the government pension started; and fourth, obviously, to seek occasional work in charing.[13] Except for the continued domestic work of keeping house for a relative or charing, the future of an older servant depended upon the savings she had been able to accumulate before losing employment. Thus, those servants who had been unfortunate in the kinds of positions they secured or who had not been able to save money now faced a bleak future, whereas those servants who had been most successful in taking advantage of the experience of service had mostly left the occupation to marry or to enter some other kind of job which was more skilled or required some capital.

It should not be inferred that unemployment, illness or old age confronted servants with hardships which were exceptional to the urban poor, except in one respect. Unemployment deprived servants of their key advantages, for in addition to providing housing, service moderated the strangeness of the city. Thus, unemployed servants were possibly less able to cope than other lower-class elements. The servant's savings, unless substantial, were quickly consumed by the cost of temporary lodgings and of finding another position.[14]

Even in the usual circumstances of the servant's existence, and apart from special disasters, normal family life was disrupted by the requirements of domestic service and this fact was a significant cause of the downward mobility of some servants. The 'induced promiscuity'[15] of domestic service offered the hazard of an illegitimate pregnancy. A great danger for the young female servant was the opportunity for her sexual exploitation by her employer.[16] The power which her employer exercised over her could easily be used to force sexual submission. Acquiescence by the servant, if it resulted in pregnancy or disclosure, usually meant immediate dismissal.

Since the end of the eighteenth century, illegitimate births had been increasing, most notably in urban areas.[17] Most of the unwed mothers were migrants to the city, and a typical pattern involved the domestic servant who had been seduced and then abandoned by her employer or some other male.[18] This pattern almost certainly persisted throughout the early nineteenth century when the great waves of urban migration brought many more young women into the cities and into domestic service. Statistics on illegitimate births in Paris in the 1880s confirm the fact that servants represented the largest *per capita* group of unwed mothers; they constituted 45 per cent of mothers who gave birth in public hospitals (Table 6.2). As Henry Mayhew commented about English servants, 'the servants often give themselves up to the sons [of families for whom they work], or to the policeman on the beat, or to soldiers in the Parks; or else to shopmen, whom they may meet in the street. Female servants are far from being a virtuous class.'[19]

Whether the servant-mother was married or unmarried, the birth of her child often meant an end to her career in service. For unmarried mothers, the cost which the birth imposed upon her could be too much for her to bear, since she had to find a nurse for her child. The nurse's services in France cost about 40 francs the first month and 25 francs thereafter.[20] In other words, the whole of the female servant's wages for months could be consumed by the cost of a wet nurse.[21] The psychic cost to the mother could be at least as high: the servant could rarely see her child and she probably knew that the mortality rate among infants sent to wet nurses was very extensive.[22] In some cases,

Table 6.2. Illegitimate births in Parisian hospitals 1883-1886

	Total Servant Births in Hospitals	Servants' % of Total Births	Servants' % of Illegitimate Births
1883	2,381	39.3	46.7
1884	2,310	37.4	43.3
1885	2,347	37.6	44.6
1886	2,471	39.5	44.8

	Civil status of servant mothers in Paris*		
	Single	Married	Widowed
1883	84.8%	13.6%	1.7%
1884	79.1	16.7	4.2
1885	79.3	17.0	3.7
1886	78.8	19.3	1.9

Source: *Annuaire statistique de la ville de Paris*, 1883, p.215; 1884, p.171; 1885, p.191; 1886, p.185.

*The declining percentage of unmarried mothers was partially due to the growing percentage of day workers in the servant population. These women were generally married since they did not live in, but they constituted the poorest class of servants, which explains their entry into public hospitals for childbirth. Without this group, the percentage of single mothers among servants would be 87.9% in 1883, 86.7% in 1884, 84.1% in 1885, and 85.4% in 1886.

it was simple infanticide to send a child to a wet nurse, but a mother had no other option if she had to continue working to support herself.

The birth of an illegitimate child did not necessarily lead to disaster for a servant. Juliette Sauget gave birth to a child out of wedlock but later married an artisan and trained herself for a skilled position.[23] Indeed, this kind of behaviour, although unacceptable to middle-class employers, was not necessarily discordant with the traditional values of rural-born individuals who became servants in order to improve their marital opportunities. Servants were generally single people who had recently migrated to the cities and their agricultural backgrounds made them expect that their relationships with the men they met would result in marriage. They were simply following the rural pattern, that had developed at least since the eighteenth century, of consummating the relationship during the courting period.[24] But because the men they met were more mobile (as in the case of soldiers) than farmers' sons and an urban society was more fluctuating and difficulties were imposed by the job of a live-in domestic, the birth of a child might intervene before the marriage could be arranged. Fantasies about marriage to one of the sons of the employer were not inconceivable either, as is suggested by several nineteenth-century novels. So the simple fact of illegitimacy need not indicate the servant's alienation or any lowering of moral standards. By defying middle-class norms in this way, servants earned the mistrust of the employer class and often suffered unfortunate consequences but did not necessarily jeopardise their own futures. Moreover, in so far as servants bearing illegitimate children were not simply raped, their behaviour related to a general change in sexual culture being expressed by the propertyless lower classes throughout western Europe and the United States in the nineteenth century.[25]

Servants' sexual behaviour was a frequent concern of nineteenth-century moralisers because the domestic servant class was clearly the greatest supplier of prostitutes, in addition to having the most illegitimate births.[26] The burden of the birth of a child for a single woman led some servants to prostitution as a means of survival in the city.[27] In fact, the revelation of any kind of sexual irregularity on the part of a servant could result in the servant's dismissal from her position.[28] This dismissal and consequent desperation of the servant was blamed for most of the prostitution of London in 1816 by London's chief of police.[29] 'It is certain,' wrote a contemporary, 'that in the great cities . . . household service has become synonymous with the worst degradation that comes to women.'[30]

But prostitution did not necessarily immerse the ex-servant in the world of the disreputable and criminal poor; the prostitute was not inevitably downwardly mobile. Even a young servant with high aspirations for making a good marriage could rationally choose prostitution as the means for more rapidly accumulating the dowry she would need. Prostitution often offered better earnings than domestic service, and was certainly more lucrative than piece-work or garment-making. Through prostitution, an individual could break away from family control which often continued when a young woman took a domestic position, and thus prostitution allowed greater personal autonomy than servanthood.[31] Though abhorrent to middle-class culture, prostitution played a very ambiguous role in the lives of urban lower-class women in the nineteenth century. As in the case of illegitimacy rates, prostitution is difficult to interpret. Here, the reasons why some servants turned to prostitution are crucial, but by no means easy to divine.

A profile of the women registered as prostitutes with the Parisian police about 1830 revealed that the majority of prostitutes were recent migrants to the city from the provinces, and many had experienced an initial seduction and been abandoned by their seducers.[32] The largest occupational group among the prostitutes were household servants — 27.9 per cent of the total, although this may have included some agricultural domestics.[33] When asked to state the reason they became prostitutes, 33 percent of the respondents listed the cause as seduction by their masters and dismissal from service.[34] Servants were indeed the focus of the sexual fantasies of men of a higher class, as the author of *My Secret Life* commented in explaining his own very numerous sexual conquests of servants and other working girls.[35]

An early twentieth-century investigation into prostitution in London came to similar conclusions. The report's author noted the 'overwhelming preponderance' of ex-domestic servants among prostitutes: of 830 prostitutes surveyed, 293 had been domestic servants.[36] Their reasons for becoming prostitutes were much more diverse than those of the earlier French prostitutes, and less than one in ten listed the reason as the loss of a good reference through sexual irregularity.[37] The differences between the two studies are not great from a statistical standpoint, despite the great increase in occupations for women other than domestic service. It was true that by the beginning of the twentieth century, the employer-servant relationship was changing, and this may account for the differences in the explanation of an otherwise persistent pattern.

While cautiously refraining from assigning a greater level of sexual 'temptations' to service over industrial work, the British Women's Industrial Council in 1916 also noted the clear connection between servanthood and prostitution.[38] In spite of the changing position of domestic servants in the course of the nineteenth century, it is obvious that domestic service constituted the path to prostitution for some female urban migrants.

Linked in another way to the high rate of illegitimate births, and probably prostitution, was the high rate of infanticide among servants. Rather than face the disgrace and dismissal which the birth of a child could impose, the servant-mother would attempt to destroy the child to eliminate the evidence of her crime against social mores. The burden which an illegitimate child imposed was so great that many servant-mothers apparently took this drastic action. The largest group of mothers in France who committed infanticide, according to available statistics, were household servants.[39] Obviously, figures on this kind of crime are not totally reliable, but servants had many reasons for wanting to rid themselves of children.[40] *L'Avenir des Femmes* in 1877 reported the case of a nineteen-year-old servant accused of infanticide. She had been seduced by her employer and he had refused to help her when she realised that she was pregnant. Consequently, the girl killed her child immediately after his birth.[41] Infanticide was used as a form of birth control when other means failed or were unknown and the burden of an unwanted child seemed too great to bear. A less direct, but equally effective, method of eliminating this burden was to send the child to one of the wet nurses or foundling homes from whose care no infants survived.[42] This kind of institutionalised infanticide was effective in controlling births, and was less hazardous for the mother than the killing of her own infant. The high rate of infanticide, whether direct or surreptitious, underlines the desperation with which many servants faced the not-uncommon prospect of the birth of an illegitimate child.

Because illegitimate births involved many servants in criminal activities like infanticide and prostitution, the illegitimacy rates among servants seemed to confirm employers' complaints about servants' immorality and criminality. So whatever the real explanation of these phenomena is, servants' behaviour was often clearly unacceptable to the middle classes. However accurate the resulting complaints in describing servant behaviour, the fears of employers could colour and distort the master-servant relationship even when no indecorum was involved.

Employers' complaints about servants' immorality also included comments on drunkenness and thefts. Servant alcoholism and theft are not unexpected given the conditions of most of their lives, the amount of degradation which some had to endure in service, and the lower-class backgrounds from which marginal servants like charwomen came. Servants may have indicated their alienation from their work through the excessive use of alcohol and stealing from their employers. Drunkenness was allegedly the most characteristic problem of servants. Studies of alcoholism in nineteenth-century France are full of stories of drunken cooks and footmen.[43] A popular image of the English charwoman was that of a gossip and a drunk.[44] The manuals warned employers that this problem was the result of the wine or beer allowance which gave the servant easy access to the supply.[45] Separated from their families and from frequent contacts with their friends, working in an often-hostile environment, servants may have used drinking as a means of coping with their lack of freedom and their loneliness. The drinking habits of servants were thus an important index of their disaffection, if an unquantifiable one.

Servants also defied their employers by stealing from them. The niggardliness of some employers in the quality of the food and housing which they provided for their servants encouraged domestic larceny.[46] Servants began to consider some dishonest practices, such as the 'sou pour livre' or 'poundage', as perquisites. If domestic thefts were prevalent however, as employers complained they were, actual prosecutions for such thefts were rare. Between 1820 and 1835, the greatest number of thefts in this category in Paris according to police records was 219 in one year – the equivalent of only 0.4 per cent of the total number of servants in Paris.[47] And it is likely that servants were more often accused of thefts than actually committed them. In 1900 in France, of those servants accused of domestic thefts, nearly half of them were acquitted.[48] Servants were probably not an exceptionally larcenous group, although some kinds of dishonest practices to which employers objected were undoubtedly quite common. Nor did theft spell disaster for a servant's future. Petty thefts, if undiscovered, could fatten a servant's bank account and hasten movement into a better situation.

High rates of infanticide, prostitution, and some tendency to theft by servants combined to give the impression of a high level of criminality among servants, but this was largely unjustified. Crime statistics, which show that servants on the average committed a greater percentage of the crimes than was warranted by their percentage of the population, were generally based on records of indictments rather than on convictions, and servants had a high rate of acquittal. Because they were easily accused and easily caught, servants were more likely to be charged for such crimes as theft. Even at this level of accusation, servants' crimes were usually not of the most vicious sort; they were more characteristically types of crimes which reflected a certain degree of disaffection with their situation, such as domestic stealing (which was usually petty larceny, not a major theft). Infanticide had long been a widely-used, though illegal, form of birth control when other methods failed, particularly in France. Prostitution was probably at worst the only option of an unskilled woman, desperate for work, who no longer had the proper references to secure further domestic employment. There were relatively few serious crimes of servants against their employers, though the ones which did occur received considerable publicity. The sensationalised 'crime of the rue de Sèze' in Paris in the 1880s, for instance, was caused by a valet who had murdered his wealthy widowed mistress for fear that his thefts from her would be discovered.[49] Because servants were considered to be the holders of a sacred trust, however, and more prosaically because of their physical proximity, however, employers were more sensitive to the possibility of crimes they might commit. Employers feared, for example, that the high rate of infanticides by servants meant that servants possessed some malicious intent toward children and that their own children might be abused by servants, though there is no evidence that attacks by domestics against children occurred except very rarely.[50] Thus, servants belonged to the criminal milieu only exceptionally – and these were largely unemployed domestics and prostitutes. But the image of criminality cannot be ignored. It may have lowered middle-class interest in employing a servant by the late nineteenth century. It might also have encouraged the servant eager for respectability to seek a different career. And it must have embittered relations between a mistress and her servant.

In terms of actual behaviour, however, it is unfortunately impossible to sketch more than an impressionistic picture of the misery which some servants experienced and to evaluate the degree to which that misery was different from other lower-class groups and produced distinctive behaviour. Servants seem to have suffered more severely than other groups but this is because they made more frequent use of public institutions. Because of the traditional lower-class distrust of public institutions, most lower-class groups avoided these institutions even in their direst misery. Servants, on the other hand, perhaps because of their contacts with the middle classes or because they were cut off from family contacts, were less reluctant to seek help when they were ill or destitute. Certainly servants, because they had no home outside the household in which they worked and because they worked in an isolated situation, undoubtedly had fewer kin and friendship networks on which to draw when disaster struck. Servant-mothers were more likely than others to commit themselves to public hospitals to bear their illegitimate children, and servants were also more often admitted to the public hospitals of Paris for other reasons. In 1826, 5 per cent of those admitted to public hospitals in Paris were servants; in 1829, this percentage was 7 per cent, or two to three times the percentage of servants in the city's population.[51] French servants also accounted for a disproportionate percentage of the total of suicides.[52] Although the causes of suicide are obviously much too complex to be related to one cause, servants' alienation from their occupation may have accounted for part of their greater propensity to commit suicide than the norm. English commentators also noted the high percentage of ex-servants in female penitentiaries and hospitals in the nineteenth century.[53] In the reports of the parishes of London in 1834 for the Poor Law Report, 26 out of the 40 parishes responding listed domestic servants as the group most subject to distress in that particular parish.[54] Thus, the conclusion is inescapable that some servants suffered significantly and visibly in spite of some of the advantages of their occupations.

Paradoxically, one of the sources of servants' disaffection was their interaction with middle-class aspirations for social mobility which aroused expectations in the servants which for many remained unfulfilled. Heightened expectations clashed with the disillusioning realities of poor housing, long hours, lack of freedom, mistreatment, and the debasing experience of the deference which service often required. When the servant experienced the tension between expectation and reality, there were several typical responses: the servant who was 'unruly'; the servant who left domestic service for another occupation, or simply changed positions frequently; the servant who expressed resentment collectively; and the servant who internalised the conflict and reflected the psychological stress in drinking, theft or, at the extreme, suicide or serious crime. As has been indicated, collective action was the least frequent response of disaffected servants. Most often, servants either did not experience undue tension or reacted to it by changing jobs within the service sector, by defying employers' expectations, or by leaving domestic service. The tremendous mobility within domestic service allowed job tensions to be worked out by changing positions or at least to be endured because the occupation was considered only temporary.

One of the ways in which servants vented their frustrations without endangering their future plans was to defy middle-class values and authority. A clear case of servant resentment of middle-class standards related to the obsessive concern of some employers about the security of their possessions and their fear of domestic thefts. Jean Rennie, an English kitchen maid, recalled in her autobiography the manner in which her mistress had tried to catch her servants in dishonest activity.[55] One day in cleaning the billiards room, Rennie found a half-crown on the carpet, and under the rug were spread out an entire deck of cards; the former to test her honesty, the latter to test her diligence in cleaning. Rennie responded to the implied insult by glueing cards and coin to the floor. Though unwilling to be 'branded a rebel', Rennie refused to bear the indignity of this kind of treatment. In a similar rebellion Margaret Powell simply declined to wear the uniform white cuffs and cap of a cook which her mistress provided in the hope of making her look more like a servant.[56] Such behaviour may have made employers so uncomfortable that they ultimately decided against employing servants by the end of the nineteenth century.

As should be clear by now, social mobility, both upward and downward, depended heavily on servants' mentality. The element of chance was important — in the form of the character of the employer, the specific working conditions, and the ease of placement. But some servants succeeded at least in part because of the initial decision to migrate a great distance, out of a desire for a better life — 'to better myself, mum', as Lilian Westall, a seventeen-year-old housemaid expressed it to her employer.[57] Debasement was partly a matter of accepting the employers' disdain of their servants. By defying the assumption of inferiority, as Jean Rennie did in refusing to allow her employers to test her honesty, servants often did not experience the debasement. Servants had many ways of making the lives of their employers difficult and even unpleasant, and they used this means to counter the system of deference and its debilitating effects. The 'good' servant in the middle-class perspective, was docile and malleable, but the successful one may have been quite different. How much servants realised options and evaluated advantages and disadvantages in a calculating way had much to do with upward and downward mobility and the feelings they had about their work. This question of mentality remains a fascinating one which has no simple answer.

In sum, the question of mobility is crucial for understanding domestic service in the nineteenth century. Although difficult to assess accurately, the fact of mobility is integral to the experience of individual servants, for most people experienced service as a temporary occupation — the movement was up and out or down and out, but nearly always out. Both the downwardly mobile and disaffected and the sometimes defiant but upwardly mobile elements helped to define the transitional character of domestic service in the age of industrialisation.

7. PROGRESS AND DECLINE

The rise and decline of domestic service constituted a distinct phase in the modernisation of western societies. As has already been outlined, the rise of servanthood as an important urban activity accompanied the accelerated urbanisation of the late eighteenth to the mid-nineteenth century. The increase in servants is not difficult to explain, given the increasingly numerous urban middle classes, their rising wealth, and the need for domestic help in coping with the dirt and unpleasantness of the early industrial city. But a more problematic and fascinating question is the decline of servanthood in the twentieth century, and this question reflects not simply on the occupation itself but on broader social changes, the increasing occupational opportunities for women, and the evolution of new values in both the middle and working classes.

After 1880 in France and 1890 in England, the growth of the total servant class slowed. In France, the number of servants declined both absolutely and in percentage terms. The decline in France was clear before the end of the nineteenth century, but it did not constitute a dramatic change until after the First World War (Table 7.1). In England, the increase in the servant population also levelled off after 1890, and in terms of their proportion of the British labour force, servants began to decline. As in France, the significant turning-point was the First World War, although the depression of the 1930s brought many women back into the domestic labour force to supplement declining family incomes. Table 7.1 clearly indicates that the era of the First World War witnessed the end of the middle-class live-in servant.

But the overall numbers of servants conceal the more significant alterations which were occurring in domestic employment. The whole character of domestic service was changing in the first two decades of the twentieth century. Although service continued to be the major occupier of women until 1940 throughout Western Europe and the United States, the middle-class employment of live-in domestics had ended by 1920. Younger women were now following the earlier male pattern of taking advantage of other job opportunities as they began to recognise the declining advantages of servanthood. Instead, the numbers of the servant class were swelled by an increasing percentage of day workers. Hence, the real revolution took place beneath the surface of the total numbers.

The phenomenon of the shrinking domestic labour force focuses our attention on three groups which were involved in this revolution. First were those who still found in domestic work a refuge — older women of the lower classes who could find occasional employment as

111

Table 7.1. Total servant populations in France and England,
Rates of Increase and Decrease, 1851-1931

	France		England	
	Total	% Increase or Decrease	Total	% Increase or Decrease
1851	906,666	–	908,138	–
1861	896,952	– 1.1	1,123,428	+23.7
1871	949,269	+ 5.8	1,387,872	+23.5
1881	1,156,604	+21.8	1,453,175	+ 4.7
1891	925,892	–19.9	1,549,502	+ 6.6
1901	956,195	+ 3.3	1,370,773	–11.5
1911	929,548	– 2.8	1,314,024	– 2.2
1921	787,385	–15.3	1,209,704	– 7.9
1931	–	–	1,410,713	+ 16.6*

Source: *Statistique générale de la France* and *Census of England and Wales.*

*Note the increase in domestic servants during the depression. Charing also increased between the First World War and the 1930s, suggesting that these were mainly women who went to work to supplement family incomes in a period of crisis.

charwomen. Second were the middle-class mistresses whose motivations and expectations had an important effect on servant employment. And third, there were the younger women who had previously gone into service but now were not.

The increasing number of older servants indicates that a growing number of women were seeking domestic jobs after many years of child-rearing or as the result of widowhood. This was partially due to increased longevity which increased the probability of widowhood among women. After 1890, the percentage of servants who were married or widowed and over the age of forty-five was very gradually rising.[1]

Most of the older women were part of the class of charwomen or 'femmes de ménage' who were employed on a daily or occasional basis and did not live in. At the end of the nineteenth century, daily workers in France constituted only 8 percent of the total number of domestics although *femmes de ménages* were proportionately more numerous in Paris – about 11 per cent of the total there.[2] But even this small number of non-resident servants was undoubtedly larger than it had been earlier in the nineteenth century. In England in 1851, charwomen numbered only 55,000 in a servant population of nearly a million (Table 7.2). London, like Paris, attracted more charwomen; there they constituted 7 per cent of the total indoor servant population.[3] After 1880, the number of daily workers showed a persistent increase.[4] Thus, while the bulk of household servants remained live-in domestics until the early twentieth century, their majority was rapidly diminishing in favour of non-resident domestics.

The increase in daily servants at the beginning of the twentieth century responded to the need for domestic labour which was no longer supplied by live-in help. And charing was clearly an occupation for older women who were or had been married (Table 7.3).[5] We cannot be sure what women in this category had done in the period before the 1890s when domestic work was largely the preserve of younger single women. The older women may have worked at other kinds of occasional work or not worked at all after marriage, and charing may have been an important opportunity to ameliorate their economic situation. We know so little about older women that it is difficult to assess the significance of charing in individual experience. But, as we have noted earlier, the working life of lower-class women often followed a cyclic pattern; occasional or temporary work was sought in depressed times to augment family income when the husband's wage was inadequate or nonexistent. Older servants may also have continued to work as dailies rather than face the bleak prospect of retirement on an insubstantial pension or paltry savings.[6] Older, more traditionally-minded women thus continued to find charing an acceptable occupation, and its accessibility was increased with the outflow of younger workers.

Table 7.2. Charwomen in England and Wales, Rates of Increase and Decrease

	Total	% of Servant Class	% Increase or Decrease
1851	55,423	6.0	
1861	65,273	6.3	+ 17.8
1871	77,650	6.1	+ 18.9
1881	92,474	7.0	+ 19.0
1891	104,808	7.0	+ 13.3
1901	111,841	7.5	+ 6.7
1911	126,061	9.1	+ 12.7
1921	118,476	8.9	− 6.0
1931	140,146	9.9	+ 18.3

Source: *Census of England and Wales.*

The decline of live-in domestic servants was also due to the decisions of middle-class mistresses in whose households servants would have been employed. By the end of the nineteenth century, the middle classes were dissatisfied with the institution of live-in domestic service and were beginning to make the difficult choice not to employ a live-in

Table 7.3. Ages of charwomen in England and Wales, 1851-1911

	1851 %	1861 %	1871 %	1881 %	1891 %	1911 %
Under 20	2.8	2.1	2.2	2.1	2.8	1.6
20-34	20.8	19.8	19.4		18.7	
				41.7		40.9
35-44	22.3	22.6	23.0		24.6	
45-54	24.5	23.9	24.6		26.0	
				45.5		48.5
55-64	18.1	18.8	18.8		18.4	
65-	11.4	12.4	12.4	10.7	9.5	9.0
Percentage of Chars Over 45	54.0	55.4	55.8	56.2	53.9	57.5

Source: *Census of England and Wales.*

maid. This decision was not simply the result of rising rents and food prices, although reference has already been made to the significant effects of inflation on middle-class budgets in this period.[7] The fact that the decline in live-in servants went unheralded by discernible competitive bidding for the remaining domestics (and hence by rising servant wages) indicates that the middle-class desire to employ servants was also waning.[8] As we have suggested, the middle-class emphasis on domesticity was becoming increasingly expressed as a closeness and exclusiveness which could no longer tolerate an obtrusive stranger.

The middle-class experience with servants in the nineteenth century had been full of tensions. Numerous accusations of servant criminality and immorality embittered employer-servant relationships, leading to employer mistrust and servant defiance.[9] Some middle-class housewives must have tired of the crude and sometimes raucous behaviour of servants. The declining birth rate also had an effect on middle-class choices by the late nineteenth century. Because they now had fewer children to care for, the English middle classes, like the French, had less need of a servant.[10] Thus, the middle-class family was turning inward just as the servant was developing a desire for independence and a clash of values was inevitable.

This clash of values was felt very much by the servants themselves, but it was only one reason for the choice against service which was being made by increasing numbers of young single women in the years of the early twentieth century. The very young were no longer employed in service after 1900 since the educational system's expansion had cut into the under-fifteen population. In England, where the pubescent servant had been much more common than in France, there were still 22,588

114

children under fourteen employed as servants in 1901.[11] By 1911 less than 8,000 remained in service in this age group.[12] Education not only kept the very young out of the labour force, but it also provided them with the basic skills which expanded their occupational options.

The expansion of public schools cannot, however, explain the decline in employment of individuals above the school age. Between 1881 and 1901 there was a 7.3 per cent drop in the proportion of servants between fifteen and nineteen years of age.[13] This drop clearly suggests that the individuals who earlier would have been servants were recognising other employment options. The educational systems were helping to close the rural-urban gap and they also were providing a new channel for the occupational mobility of young men and women. The profession of primary school teaching could, like domestic service, act as a bridging occupation:[14] the occupation involved training, geographical mobility and delay of marriage, so that for some individuals this occupation filled the role formerly played by domestic service.

Even more important, after 1880, the growth of a larger white-collar class provided an important new source of feminine employment as a respectable, though temporary, occupation for a young woman before marriage.[15] As with teaching, the jobs of shop assistant or clerical worker provided the service roles which women are still socialised to perform. The attractiveness of other occupations contrasts sharply with the diminishing interest in domestic service.

The decline of live-in domestics raises a question about that segment of the rural population which earlier in the nineteenth century would have become servants. In the first place, this segment was obviously smaller than before, and the declining birth rate in the countryside was easing the pressure on the land which had pushed many into service earlier.[16] But those who did migrate were being acculturated by some other means. The schools accomplished a certain degree of general acculturation and the rural-born individuals who moved to the cities had often already acquired an urban outlook. By 1900, the completed transportation and communication networks had begun to destroy rural isolation even in an incompletely urbanised country like France.[17] Substantial urbanisation also meant that more servants would have to be recruited from the urban lower classes to maintain the size of the servant class. The urban-born had always been more reluctant to become servants.[18] The freer atmosphere of the city bred a greater distaste for the lack of freedom which service involved, and urban-born women did not experience the cycle of early agricultural service which channelled the rural-born into household service.

From the middle of the eighteenth century until the early twentieth century, urban household service offered young single women a kind of employment which fulfilled all the traditional expectations women had for work. Domestic service preserved the familial context for work and did not initially require a wrenching change from previous experience. Yet urban servanthood established an urban work pattern for women — it did not require a permanent commitment to the occupation and the servant could expect at least the freedom to change positions frequently if she wished.

Until late in the nineteenth century, domestic service provided unique economic advantages which made it particularly attractive. But as these advantages waned, as we have already discussed,[19] the servant class also dwindled, raising again the question of servants' occupational expectations. How much had servants ever really wanted to be servants? How clearly had they understood the economic advantages, as opposed to simply accepting a traditional role? The answers may lie in the kinds of work which women entered in the early twentieth century.

As service employment declined, white-collar jobs became increasingly important. White-collar employment was less physically demanding than either factory work or domestic service. It was also socially respectable; a young clerical worker did not have to disguise her occupation in fancy clothing when she went out, as the servant did.[20] The shop assistant or banker's clerk had greater personal independence — contrasted with the often-repeated complaint of the urban servant. As domestics acquired the middle-class values of self-determination and self-discipline, their desire for autonomy undoubtedly increased and the need for a familial context diminished. But women maintained their preference for a more personal work relationship. The opportunity to meet people and to socialise on the job with co-workers replaced the personal relationship of the servant to her employer. Thus, domestic service had reinforced some of the most pervasive feminine attitudes toward work, while contributing to the modernisation of women's work.

The declining economic advantages of servanthood, the slowing of urban migration, the evolution of the middle-class family ethic, and the adoption of an urban work ethic by the rural-born all contributed to the changing nature of domestic service by the early twentieth century. Once the most pervasive common experience of rural-born individuals, and particularly of lower-class women, domestic service became the source of occasional employment for the destitute and unskilled. Except in areas like the emerging nations of Latin America, where the earlier European pattern is now being repeated, domestic service has retreated to a marginal role in the economies of most western societies and no longer plays a significant role in the training or work experience of the modern woman.

8. CONCLUSION

The modernisation of the economy meant the transfer of the production of goods outside of the home and the commercialisation of services. Domestic servants became confined to those tasks which resisted mechanisation and commercialisation, at least temporarily. Widespread employment of domestics thus tended to slow the rationalisation of household work and to hinder the development of the commercial sector to handle a variety of unspecialised household chores.[1] Viewed in this way, domestic service impeded the modernisation of the economy and seems to have no place in the history of an industrialising and urbanising economy. Yet it should be clear at this point that domestic service, seen in human terms, had a key function in this economic and social evolution. On the one hand, the employment of servants initiated the middle-class woman into the role of employer/manager and initiated her into certain professional skills. On the other hand, for the servants themselves, service had a significant impact on the distribution of the labour supply and was an important channel for urban migration. Almost paradoxically, domestic service served as a means of the modernisation of rural labour and particularly of women.

Domestic service has played a similar role in all of the western societies, yet that role has reflected the specific characteristics of particular patterns of industrialisation. For example, the peculiarities of the low French birth rate and of the French inheritance and land-tenure laws slowed the evolution of large-scale industrial enterprises to the advantage of more traditional occupations so that a larger variety of home industries was available to women workers in France than was the case for female workers in England and elsewhere. Moreover, the labour shortage gave French workers an advantage over English workers in higher wages and more plentiful occupational opportunities. Comparing France to England and other western countries, only the United States fits the labour-short pattern of France.

In addition to the limited supply of free labour, the early drop in the French birth rate produced a very small middle-class family early in the nineteenth century. The British middle-class family, although beginning to limit births by mid-century, did not experience a significant decline in family size until later in the nineteenth century.[2] The smaller French middle-class family had less need for a large household staff, and even at mid-century, the average French middle-class family employed only a single female servant. Among English servant-employing families, the average number of servants employed was

1.8.³ At the end of the nineteenth century, the servant elements in England and Germany were considerably larger than in France as a percentage of total population, and only the United States had a lower servant ratio than France (Table 8.1).⁴ But in the first two decades of the twentieth century, the national patterns were beginning to converge.

Table 8.1. Servants' percentage of total population

	1901 %	1911 %
Great Britain	4.13	3.77
Germany	3.12 (1895)	2.66 (1907)
France	2.45	2.35
United States	1.98	2.03 (1910)

Source: George Stigler, *Domestic Servants in the United States, 1900-1940* (New York: National Bureau of Economic Research, Occasional Paper, No.24, 1946), p.4.

Throughout this study an effort has been made to emphasise the comparative analysis of England and France in order to construct a model of the role of domestic service in industrialising societies. The model which has emerged is that urban domestic service encouraged the movement of young peasants into the cities, often facilitated their settlement there, and provided rural-born women in particular with a useful and respectable occupation before marriage. Servanthood declined in importance after urbanisation had peaked and after occupational opportunities for young women expanded. Live-in domestic service constituted an acculturation process which declined when the need for such acculturation waned.

But the vital similarities between the English and French patterns of the evolution of domestic service should not lead us to ignore the equally significant differences. England was more highly urbanised and more heavily industrialised than France. The urbanisation and feminisation of the English servant class occurred earlier, indicating the greater economic and demographic pressures on the countryside there. So that it is not surprising that young Englishwomen were forced into domestic service at an earlier age than their French sisters. And somewhat more English servants were drawn from the urban populations than in France. Finally, proportionately fewer French women were employed in factories than their English counterparts, although more Frenchwomen were employed overall, most of them in a variety of home industries and in agriculture.

Clearly, the experience of servanthood was not identical for English and French women, although it was similar. The more traditional, land-based society in France lent greater weight to the wages of a servant, whether they were sent home to her family or accumulated for a dowry; it also encouraged higher wages which might push servants toward new attitudes. More complete modernisation was apparent, in the master-servant relationship in England, where the paternalistic relationship was already giving way to a contractual arrangement early on in the nineteenth century. The French middle classes were more likely to complain of contemporary servants and cling to their image of the faithful retainer who could be considered a member of the family.

In some important respects, the case of the United States confirms the model already suggested, in spite of important differences with both the French and English experiences. Like France, the United States in the nineteenth century had a labour-short economy, and domestic servants were largely a migrant group. But in the U.S., unlike the European countries, the majority of domestic servants were foreign-born or non-white.[5] But despite this fact, American servants, like their European sisters, enjoyed a distinct wage advantage over other female workers. An investigation by the U.S. Department of Labor at the end of the nineteenth century revealed that the average annual earnings of urban working women were less than those of domestic servants when time lost was considered.[6] But even in England, where a labour shortage cannot be used to explain the competitive wages of servants, the compensation for service was sufficiently attractive to act as a motivation for selecting domestic work.[7]

Without denying the differences among national groups of servants, then, it is clear that servants shared more with their counterparts than with other kinds of workers in their native countries. Servanthood was a cross-cultural experience of immense significance. The pattern of rapid expansion and later contraction of the size of the servant population was common to western Europe and the United States during the nineteenth and early twentieth centuries. The same pattern is being repeated in many Latin American countries in the mid-twentieth century. This pattern results from the basic fact that domestic service is an occupation central to the transition from a purely familial economy to an industrial mass-production economy. Middle-class women, as already noted, needed domestic help in the struggle to create a clean, comfortable and respectable atmosphere for their families in a nineteenth-century city. Lower-class women, some purely out of tradition, preferred the work in middle-class households.

During its peak, the influence of domestic service was much more extensive than it may seem precisely because of its role in acculturation. The experience of a term in service inevitably coloured the lives of a large segment of the generations before 1914 throughout western Europe. A quarter of all French and English women probably served as domestics for a period of time in the nineteenth century. French domestics, urban and rural, constituted one in every 2·9 French women who were single between the ages of 15 and 49 in 1851, and one of every 2·4 single women in 1881.[8] In 1851 in England, one in every five women, aged 15 to 30, was listed as a domestic, and here we are dealing with urban situations alone.[9] Moreover, through marriage, the experience of a former female servant was communicated to her family so that the effects of her training could be multiplied. In this way the experience of servanthood touched the lives of a wide segment of the lower classes before 1914. One of the open questions in dealing with the evolution of working-class culture in the nineteenth century is the impact of the more pervasive, better-articulated middle-class ideals. Probably pious tracts and even many kinds of schooling had less impact than we would imagine. But through the women, servant-trained and imbued with some middle-class values, the contact could be very real.

In sum, household servants in the industrialising western societies played a key role in several ways. The impact on the employing class should not be ignored, although this has not been our primary stress. The strain of dealing with girls who, in middle-class terms, were ignorant and irresponsible may well have contributed to durable class attitudes. Indeed, as we have suggested, the servant experience may have encouraged women to a new privatisation of family life in a desire to avoid difficult strangers residing in their homes. It would be interesting to compare women's complaints about their own daily contacts with a lower-class individual, comments about servants' immorality or brashness, with those of their husbands or fathers about the 'undeferential' behaviour of their employees, for men alone do not shape class antagonisms. But this is no simple topic, for bonds could be formed, training provided, that would decisively alter the life of the servant and perhaps enlighten the mistress as well.

For the servant class itself, domestic work was the middle stage for women employed outside their own homes, allowing work within a familial environment and often benefiting the servants' own families. Service was also the transitional occupation by which thousands of individuals effected the movement into the cities and into marriage or other occupations. Yet for all its traditional characteristics, service was changing in the nineteenth century and with it the work experience of thousands of rural-born individuals, and especially the working life of women. Modern servanthood initiated servants into an urban work pattern. For women more than for men, their occupation was not a lifetime commitment and the particular position could be changed for self-improvement or simply out of frustration or boredom with a particular job. Women's work experience was both more temporary and more personal than men's, and both of these aspects were embodied in the experience of servanthood. Women sought in domestic service a personal relationship with their employers and gave up domestic service only when they found this element in other occupational opportunities or when this factor was otherwise provided. In other words, domestic service, though transitory as a major employer of women — for a century

120

to a century and a half — embodied and undoubtedly caused many durable aspects of women's work. It was not intended as a lifelong career, but as a preparation for marriage, for which it often served admirably. It stressed human contacts, although tension was as probable as a close relationship. But this need for personal contact has been preserved in much of what women seek from very modern jobs. Most obviously, service avoided the impersonal factory, and women yielded to other employment only when non-factory urban work became abundant with the spread of white-collar jobs. The servant is gone, save for imports from more distant areas, but the impact of servanthood may linger. Certainly for the nineteenth century, domestic servanthood may be the best way of getting at the initial work experience and life cycle of a wide spectrum of working-class and peasant women in the period of industrialisation and urbanisation.[10]

BIBLIOGRAPHY

Books, articles, theses

Abbot, Mary, *A Woman's Paris,* Boston, 1900.
Académie française, Institut de France, *Séances publiques annuelles,*
　1851-1913.
Adams, Samuel and Sarah, *The Complete Servant,* London, 1825.
Allem, Maurice, *La vie quotidienne sous le Second Empire,* Paris, 1948.
Allix, André, *Un pays de haute-montagne. L'Oisans,* Paris, 1930.
Almanach des mystères des bureaux et agences de placement dévoilés,
　Paris, n.d.
Alq, Louise (Alquié de Rieusseyroux), *Le maître et la maîtresse de
　maison,* Paris, 1882.
Anderson, Michael, *Family Structure in Nineteenth-Century
　Lancashire,* Cambridge, 1971.
Anderson, Nellie, 'A Servant's View of the Servant's Problem', *The
　National Review,* LXI (March-August, 1913), 123-127.
Archives d'anthropologie criminelle, 3 vols., Paris, 1886-1888.
Armengaud, André, *Les populations de l'est – Aquitain au début de
　l'époque contemporaine,* Paris, 1961.
Ashwell, William, *Address on the Dissolution of the Late Servants'
　Benevolent Institution,* London, 1846.
Audiger, *La maison réglée,* Paris, 1692.
Auger, Madeleine, *Condition juridique et économique du personnel
　domestique féminin,* Paris, 1935.
Avenel, Georges d', 'Le train de maison depuis sept siècles: les
　domestiques', *Revue des Deux Mondes,* VI, no.8 (April 1, 1912),
　632-655.
L'Avenir des Femmes, Monthly, 1869-1878 (Became *Le Droit des
　Femmes* in 1879).

Babeau, Albert, *Les artisans et les domestiques d'autrefois,* Paris, 1886.
[Bailleul, J. -Ch.] *Moyens de former un bon domestique,* 2nd ed., Paris,
　1814.
Baker, Lady A. S., *Our Responsibilities and Difficulties as Mistresses of
　Young Servants,* London, 1886.
Balzac, Honoré de, *Les Parisiens Comme Ils Sont, 1830-1846,* Genève,
　n.d.
Banks, J. A., *Prosperity and Parenthood,* London, 1954.
Barbary, Dr Fernand, *Semeurs de bacilles insoupçonnes; Domestiques
　en service et atteints de tuberculose à forme torpide,* Nice, 1913.

Bassinet, 'Avis présenté au nom de la Commission de surveillance et de perfectionnement de l'école professionnelle et ménagère de jeunes filles', Conseil municipal de Paris, *Rapports* no.36 (1893).

Bayard, Dr Henry, *Mémoire sur la topographie médicale des Xe, XIe arrondissements de Paris,* Paris, 1844.

Bayle-Mouillard, Elizabeth, *Manuel complet des domestiques,* Paris, 1836.

Baylis, T. Henry, *Workmen's Compensation Act, 1906, which includes Domestic Servants and Others,* London, 1907.

Bayne-Powell, Rosamond, *Housekeeping in the Eighteenth Century,* London, 1956.

Beaufreton, Maurice, 'Comment se résoudra la question des domestiques', *La Quinzaine,* LXXII (1906), 549-563.

Becci, Gabriel, *Le placement des ouvriers et employés des deux sexes et de toutes professions et la loi du 14 mars 1904,* Paris, 1906.

Beeton, Mrs Isabella. *The Book of Household Management,* London, 1861.

Belèze, Guillaume-Louis-Gustave, *Le livre des ménages; nouveau manuel d'économie domestique,* Paris, 1861.

Bellom, Maurice, *L'Assurance contre les accidents et les domestiques,* Paris, 1908.

Berkner, Lutz K., 'The Stem Family and the Development Cycle of the Present Household: An Eighteenth-Century Austrian Example', *American Historical Review,* LXXVII (April, 1972), 398-418.

Berry, Georges, 'Rapport fait au nom de la Commission du Travail', Conseil municipal de Paris, *Rapports*, no.1677 (6th legis., session of 1895).

Best, Geoffrey, *Mid-Victorian Britain, 1851-1875,* London, 1971.

Bienaymé, Gustav, 'Le Coût de la vie à Paris à diverses époques, Gages des domestiques', *Journal de la Société de Statistique de Paris,* XL (November, 1899), 366-385.

Bizard, Dr Leon and Dr Andre Morin, *La syphilis et les domestiques,* Paris, 1923.

Black, Clementina, 'The Dislike to Domestic Service', *Nineteenth-Century,* XXXVIII (January-June, 1893), 454-456.

Black, Clementina, ed., *Married Women's Work. Being the Report of an Inquiry undertaken by the Women's Industrial Council,* London, 1915.

Boissieu, Henri de, 'L'Exode des campagnards: vers les villes dans le départment de l'Ain', *La Réforme sociale,* VIII, 5th series (July-December, 1904), 833-847.

Book of Domestic Duties, The, By the Author of the Book of Matrimony, London, 1835.

Booth, Charles, *Life and Labour of the People in London,* vol.8, London, 1903.

Bosanquet, Mrs Bernard, *Rich and Poor,* London, 1908.

Bosanquet, Mrs Bernard, ed.. *Social Conditions in Provincial Towns,* London, 1912.

Boserup, Esther, *Women's Role in Economic Development,* London, 1970.

Bossard, James, *The Sociology of Child Development,* New York, 1954.

Bouniceau-Gesmon, *Domestiques et maîtres,* Paris, 1896.

Bouton, Réné, *L'infanticide, étude morale et juridique,* Paris, 1897.

Branca, Patricia, *Silent Sisterhood,* London, 1975.

Braithwaite, Richard, *Some Rules and Orders for the Government of the House of an Earl,* London, 1821.

Broom, L. and J. H. Smith, 'Bridging Occupations', *British Journal of Sociology,* XLV, no.4 (December, 1963), 321-334.

Buchez, P.-J.-B. and P.-C. Roux, *Histoire parlémentaire de la Révolution française,* Vol. II, Paris, 1834.

Budin, Pierre, *Troubles survenus chez des nourrices,* Paris, 1898.

Buguet, Henry, *Le guide des maîtres et des domestiques,* Paris, 1881.

Burnett, John, ed., *The Annals of Labour: Autobiographies of British Working-Class People, 1820-1920,* Bloomington, Ind., 1974.

Busoni, Phillipe, 'Courrier de Paris', *Illustration,* XXXIII (April 2, 1856), 210-211.

Butler, Christina, *Domestic Service. An Inquiry by the Women's Industrial Council,* London, 1916.

Cadbury, Edward with M. Cecile Matheson and George Shann, *Women's Work and Wages. A Phase of Life in an Industrial City,* London, 1906.

Campbell, Mrs Helen, *Women Wage-Workers, Their Trades and Their Lives,* Boston, 1887.

Celnart. See Bayle-Mouillard.

Chalament, R.-El, *Les Ouvrières domestiques,* Paris-Rheims, 1905.

Chaplin, David, 'Domestic Service and the Rationalisation of Household Economy', unpublished paper, Department of Sociology, Western Michigan University, November 1968.

Chaplin, David, *Private Household Economy in the United States,* Research Report for the Office of Manpower Research, U.S. Department of Labor, December 1969.

Chaplin, David, 'Domestic Service as a Family Activity and as an Occupation during Industrialisation', paper presented to the International Sociological Association, Varna, Bulgaria, September 1970.

Charbonnel, Eugène, *Étude sur le placement gratuit des employés, ouvriers, et domestiques par les bureaux municipaux de Paris,* Nancy, 1896.

Chatelain, Abel, 'La formation de la population lyonnaise, apports savoyards au XVIIIᵉ siècle', *Revue de Geographie de Lyon,* XXVI, no.3 (1951), 345-349.

Chatelain, Abel, 'Migrations et domesticité féminine urbaine en France,

XVIIIe - XXe siècles', *Revue d'histoire économique et sociale*, XLVII, no.4 (1969), 506-528.

Chatenay (Mlle), *Rapports sur l'Enseignement ménager et les Écoles ménagères*, Angers, 1909.

Chaunu, Pierre, *La civilisation de l'Europe classique*, Paris, 1970.

Chauvet, *Le travail, études morales; les domestiques*, Caen, 1896.

Chauvin, E, 'Rapport au nom de la Commission d'assurance et de prévoyance sociale', Chambre des Députés, *Impressions*, no.927 (10th legis., session of 1911).

Checkland, S.G., *The Rise of Industrial Society in England, 1815-1885*, New York, 1964.

Chevalier, Louis, *Classes laborieuses et classes dangereuses à Paris pendant la première moitié du XIXe siècle*, Paris, 1958.

Chevalier, Louis, *La formation de la population parisienne au XIXe siècle*, Paris, 1950.

Chevalier, Michael, *La vie humaine dans les Pyrénées ariégoises*, Paris, 1956.

Cilleuls, Alfred de, 'La domesticité féminine', *La Reforme sociale*, II (July-December, 1901, 5th series), 519-524.

Clémendot, P., 'Évolution de la population de Nancy de 1788 a 1815', *Contributions à l'histoire démographique de la Révolution française*, 2nd series (Paris, 1965), pp.181-220.

Clément, Henry, 'Émigrants du centre à Paris', *Réforme sociale*, X (July-December, 1885), 481-490.

Cobb, Richard, *The Police and the People. French Popular Protest, 1789-1820*, Oxford, 1970.

Cobb, Richard, *Terreur et Subsistances, 1793-1795*, Paris, 1964.

Cobb, Richard, 'The Women of the Commune', *A Second Identity. Essays on France and French History*, London, 1969, pp.221-236.

Commission des logements insalubres de Paris, *Rapport général sur les travaux de la commission pendant les années, 1862-1865*, Paris, 1866.

'Consumption and Domestic Service: The Responsibility of Mistresses by a Medical Man', *The Daily Mail*, London, October 4, 1905, p.9.

Cormenin, 'Société de patronage pour le renvoi dans leur familles des jeunes filles sans place et des femmes d'élaissées', *Annales de la Charité*, Vol. III (1847), 254-258.

Corra, Emile, *La domesticité*, Paris, 1908.

Corré, A. Dr, *Crime et Suicide*, Paris, 1891.

Cretté-Breton, Yvonne, *Mémoirs d'une bonne*, Paris, 1966.

'Cuisinier-philosophe', *Maîtres et domestiques fin-de-siècle*, Paris, 1898.

Cusenier, Marcel, *Les domestiques en France*, Paris, 1912.

Darmuzey, Maurice, *Le placement des ouvriers, employés, et domestiques en France*, Paris, 1895.

Dash, Comtesse, *Les Femmes à Paris et en province*, Paris, 1868.

Daubié, Julie, *La femme pauvre au XIXe siècle*, Paris, 1866.

Daumard, Adeline. *La Bourgeoisie parisienne de 1815 à 1848,* Paris, 1963.

Daumard, Adeline, *Les Bourgeois de Paris au XIXe siècle,* Paris, 1970, an abridged edition of the preceding work.

Daumard, Adeline, 'Une source d'histoire sociale: L'enregistrement des mutations par décès. Le XIIe arrondissement de Paris en 1820 et 1847', *Revue d'histoire économique et sociale,* XXXV (1957), 52-78.

Daumard, Adeline, 'Une référence pour l'étude des sociétés urbaines en France au XVIIIe et XIXe siècles, projet de code socio-professionel', *Revue d'histoire moderne et contemporaine,* X (1963), 185-210.

Dausset, Louis, 'Proposition relative à la création d'une diplôme et d'un cours normal d'enseignement ménager', Conseil municipal de Paris, *Rapports,* no.15 (1904).

Davidoff, Leonore, *The Best Circles. Society, Etiquette, and the Season,* London, 1973.

Davidoff, Leonore, 'Mastered for Life: Servant, Wife, and Mother in Victorian and Edwardian Britain', *Journal of Social History,* VII, no. 4 (1974), 406-428.

Deane, Phyllis and W. A. Cole, *British Economic Growth, 1688-1959,* Cambridge, England, 1967.

De Broke, Lady Marie Willoughby, 'The Pros and Cons of Domestic Service', *The National Review,* LX (September-February, 1913), 452-460.

Deguiral, René, 'Essai sur les conditions économiques, sociales et démographiques des pays de Garonne, au cours du XIXe siècle', *Revue d'histoire économique et sociale,* XXIX, no.3 (1951) 227-251.

Delorme, Marie, 'Les domestiques', *L'Enseignement ménager* (1906), pp.77-81, 128-132, 153-156, 178-180, 197-199, 227-230.

Digard, Anicet, 'Des moyens d'améliorer la condition des femmes dans les classes labourieuses', *Mémoirs de la Société des Sciences Morales et des Arts de Seine-et-Oise,* Vol. VII (1866), pp.xlvii-lxxi.

Domestic News, Published by the Domestic Servants' Insurance Society, Monthly, 1915-1920.

Domestic Service, By an old servant, London, 1917.

Domestic Service Guide, The, London, 1865.

Domestic Servants as They Are and as They Ought to be, Brighton, 1859.

Domesticité, La, Paris [1878].

Domestique, La, Paris, 1906.

Domestiques chrétiens, Les, Paris, 1828.

Domestiques d'aujourd'hui, Des, Paris, 1877.

Doncourt, A. de, *Guerre aux Petits Abus domestiques: L'Anse du panier,* Paris, n.d.

Drault, Jean, *Nos domestiques,* Tours, n.d.

Dubois, Rémy, *De la condition juridique des domestiques,* Lille, Thèse de droit, 1907.

Dufaux de la Jonchère, E. (Mlle), *Ce que les maîtres et les domestiques doivent savoir,* Paris, 1884.

Du louage des gens de service à gages, Paris, 1902.

Du Motey, Henri Renault, *L'Esclavage a Rome. Le servage au Moyen Age. La domesticité dans les temps modernes,* Douai, 1881.

Dunbar, Janet, *The Early Victorian Woman,* London, 1957.

Economy for the Single and Married, London [1845].

Edgy, *La servante,* Paris, 1905.

Édouard, R.P., *Le Foyer domestique* [1909].

Ellis, Sarah Stickney, *The Wives of England,* London [1843].

Ellis, Sarah Stickney, *The Women of England,* 2nd ed., London, 1939.

'Espoir', *How to Live on a Hundred a Year, Make a Good Appearance, and Save Money,* London, 1874.

Flaubert, Gustave, *Madame Bovary,* Paris, 1862.

Flaubert, Gustave, *Trois Contes,* Paris, 1883.

Fleury, M. and P. Valmary, 'Le Progrès de l'instruction élémentaire de Louis XIV à Napoléon III d'après l'enquête de Louis Maggiolo (1877-1879)', *Population,* XII (1957), 61-90.

Fortin, Buisson and Saint, Drs, *Rapport medico-legal sur un cas de transmission de syphilis d'un nourrisson à sa nourrice,* Paris, 1866.

Fouin, L.F., *De l'état des domestiques en France et des moyens propres à les moraliser,* Paris, 1837.

Fourastié, Jean, *Prix de vente et prix de revient,* École pratique des Hautes Etudes, 4th series, 1965.

Fourcade, Olivier, *De la condition civile des domestiques,* Paris, Thèse de droit, 1898.

Français peints par eux-mêmes, Les, 8 vols., Paris, 1840-1850.

Franklin, Alfred, *La vie privée d'autrefois,* 27 vols., Paris, 1887-1902.

Froger de l'Éguille, La Baronne de, *Manuel des domestiques,* Poiters, 1883.

Gallier, H. de, 'Comment on était servi autrefois', *La Revue,* LXXXVI (June 15, 1910), 487-501, and LXXXVII (July 1, 1910), 64-77.

Garden, Maurice, *Lyon et les Lyonnais au XVIIIe siècle,* Paris, 1971.

Gardiner, Marguerite, *The Governess,* 2 vols. London, 1939.

Gautier, Abbé Élie, *L'Emigration bretonne,* 2 vols., Paris, 1953.

Gazette des Cochers, Weekly, 1883-1884.

Gazette des Cochers et des Gens de Maison, 1887-1910.

Genlis, Comtesse de, *La Bruyère des Domestiques précédé de considerations sur l'état de domesticité en général.*

Going to Service, London, 1858.

Goncourt, Edmond de, *La Fille Elisa,* 2nd ed., Paris, 1877.

Goncourt, Edmond de and Jules de Goncourt, *Germinie Lacerteux,*

3rd ed., Paris, 1875.

Good Servants Make Good Places, London [1871].

Good Servant, The, London, 1864.

Gordon, I.M., *Mistresses and Maidservants,* London, 1884.

Granier, C., *La femme criminelle,* Paris, 1906.

Grasilier, Léonce, 'Les domestiques sous Napoleon et aujourd'hui', *La Nouvelle Revue,* LIX (1922, 4th series), 63-68.

Grégoire, Abbé Henri-Baptiste de, *De la domesticité chez les peuples anciens et modernes,* Paris, 1814.

Guichonnet, P., 'L'Émigration saisonnière en Faucigny pendant la première moitié du XIXe siècle (1793-1860)', *Revue de Géographie alpine,* XXXIII (1945), 465-534.

Guilbert, Madeleine, *Les femmes et l'organisation syndicale avant 1914,* Paris, 1966.

Guillard, Charles, 'Rapport presenté au nom de la 6e commission', Conseil municipal de Paris, *Rapports,* no.23 (1912).

Guizot, Madame, *Éducation domestique, ou lettres de famille,* 2 vols., 2nd ed., Paris, 1881.

Haas, Lucien and Eugène Penancier, *Maîtres et Gens de Service,* Paris, 1925.

Handbook of Women's Work, The, London, 1876.

Harrison, J.F.C., *The Early Victorians, 1832-1851,* London, 1971.

Haudrère, A., *Des Accidents dont sont victimes dans leur travail les domestiques et gens de maison,* Paris, 1911.

Haussonville, Othenin, 'La vie et les salaires à Paris', *Revue des Deux-Mondes,* LVI (April, 1883), 815-867.

Hecht, J. Jean, *The Domestic Servant Class in Eighteenth-Century England,* London, 1956.

Hewitt, Margaret, *Wives and Mothers in Victorian Industry,* London, 1958.

Hill, Georgiana, *Women in English Life from Medieval to Modern Times,* 2 vols., London, 1896.

Hints to Domestic Servants, By a Butler, 2nd ed., London, 1854.

Hom, Léon, *De la situation juridique des gens de service,* Paris, Thèse de droit, 1901.

Household Management, By an Old Housekeeper, London, 1877.

Household Work, or the Duties of Female Servants, London, 1850.

How to Improve the Conditions of Domestic Service, By a Servant, London, 1894.

Huber, Michel, 'Mortalité suivant la profession', *Bulletin de la Statistique générale de la France,* I (1911-1912), 402-439.

Hubscher, Ronald-Henri, 'Une contribution à la connaissance des milieux populaires ruraux au XIXe siècle. Le livre de compte de la famille Flauhaut (1811-1877),' *Revue d'histoire économique et sociale,* XLVII, no.3, (1969), 361-403.

Hudry-Menos, J., 'Le service domestique', *La Revue,* LII (1904, 4th series), 404-419.

Hufton, Olwen H., *The Poor of Eighteenth-Century France, 1750-1789,* Oxford, 1974.

Hutchins, B.L., *Statistics of Women's Life and Employment,* London, 1909.

James, Mrs Eliot, *Our Servants. Their Duties to Us and Ours to Them,* London, 1883.

Jarlin, Françoise, *Les Domestiques à Bordeaux en 1872,* Bordeaux, Travail d'Études et de Recherches, Faculté des Lettres et Sciences Humaines, University of Bordeaux, 1969.

Jean-Pierre, *Maîtres et serviteurs,* Lille, 1904.

Johnson, William, *The Servant Problem. Can It be Solved? Why Not?* London, 1922.

Jollivet, Gaston, 'Les domestiques parisiens', *Correspondant,* CCXXXII (1908), 458-475.

Jones, Gareth Stedman, *Outcast London,* London, 1971.

Jouhaud, Pierre, *Paris dans le dix-neuvième siècle,* Paris, 1809.

Journal des Gens de Maison, Monthly, 1891-1906.

Juillerat, Paul, *L'hygiène du logement,* Paris, 1909.

'Justice', *Solution of the Domestic Servant Problem,* North Shields, 1910.

Kamm, Josephine, *Hope Deferred. Girls' Education in English History,* London, 1965.

Karr, Alphonse, 'La domesticité', *Nouveau Tableau de Paris au XIXe siècle* (Paris, 1835), VI, 325-342.

Katz, Paul, *Situation économique et sociale des domestiques en France, en Allemagne et en Suisse,* Montpellier, Thèse, 1941.

'Keeping Up Appearances', *Cornhill Magazine,* IV (July-December, 1861), pp.305-318.

La Bedollière, Émile de, *Les Industriels. Métiers et professions en France,* Paris, 1842.

Lady Servants – For and Against, London, 1906.

Lafabrègue, Réné, 'Des enfants trouvés à Paris', *Annales de démographie internationale,* II (1878), 226-299.

Lamartine, Alphonse de, *Geneviève, Histoire d'une servante,* Paris, 1850.

Largeaud, E. and A. Martin, *Code-Manuel des maîtres et domestiques ou serviteurs à gages et les usages locaux du département des Deux-Sèvres,* Angers, 1911.

Lasalle, J. Henri, *Maison hospitalière. Projet d'un établissement destiné à recevoir les femmes domestiques aux époques ou elles sont sans place,* Paris, 1827.

Laslett, Peter, *The World We Have Lost,* New York, 1966.

Lavollée, Réné, 'La dépopulation des campagnes', *La Réforme sociale,*

VIII (July-December, 1904, 5th series), 345-360.

Layton, W.T., 'Changes in the Wages of Domestic Servants during Fifty Years', *Journal of the Royal Statistical Society*, LXXI (1908), 515-524.

Le Play, Frédéric, *La Reforme sociale en France*, 2 vols., Paris, 1864.

'La legende des bons vieux serviteurs', *La Liberté*, April 18, 1924.

Lesueur, Madame, *Pour Bien Tenir Sa Maison*, Paris, 1911.

Levasseur, Émile, *La population française*, 3 vols., Paris, 1889-1892.

Lewis, Mrs, *Domestic Service in the Present Day*, London, 1889.

Lewis, Elizabeth, 'A Reformation of Domestic Service', *Nineteenth Century*, XXXVIII (January-June, 1893), 127-138.

Lichtenberger, Andre, 'Nous et nos domestiques', *Conferencia* (June 15, 1925), 17-35.

Lipset, Seymour Martin and Reinhard Bendix, *Social Mobility in Industrial Society*, Berkeley, 1967.

Livre d'or des domestiques, Le, Paris, 1909.

Lochhead, Marion, *The Victorian Household*, London, 1964.

Lottin, Alain, 'Naissances illégitimes et filles-mères à Lille au XVIIIe siècle', *Revue d'histoire moderne et contemporaine*, XVII (1970), 278-322.

Lowenthal, Dr, 'État sanitaire et démographique comparée des villes de Paris et de Berlin', *Journal de la Société de Statistique de Paris*, XLVII (1906), 259-277.

Lyon, *Documents administratifs statistiques, 1881-1900*, Archives municipales de Lyon.

McCall, Mrs Dorothy Home, 'Another Aspect of the Servant Problem', *The National Review*, LX (September, 1912 – February, 1913), 969-973.

Mann, T.G., *The Duties of an Experienced Servant*, London, 1894.

Manuel des Bons Domestiques, Paris, 1896.

Marcus, Stephen, *The Other Victorians*, New York, 1964.

Massard, Emile, 'Proposition relative à l'hygiène et au travail des gens de maison', Conseil municipal de Paris, *Rapports*, no.15 (1906).

Massard, Emile, 'Proposition relative à l'hygiène des habitations de Paris en général, et en particulier des logements de concierges, gens de maison et employés logés', Conseil municipal de Paris, *Rapports*, no.96 (1909).

Mayhew, Henry, *London Labour and the London Poor*, Vol. IV, new ed., New York, 1968.

Mercier, Louis, *Tableau de Paris*, 12 vols., Amsterdam, 1782-1788.

Michelet, Jules, *La Femme*, Paris, 1860.

Mirbeau, Octave, *Le Journal d'une femme de chambre*, Paris, 1900.

Mittre, Marius-Henri-Casimir, *Des domestiques en France, dans leur rapports avec l'économie sociale, le bonheur domestique, les lois civiles, criminelles, et de police*, Paris, 1838.

Mizruchi, Ephraim Harold, 'Alienation and Anomie: Theoretical and Empirical Perspectives', *The New Sociology,* ed. Irving Horowitz, New York, 1964, pp.253-267.

Modell, John, 'The Peopling of a Working-Class Ward: Reading, Pennsylvania, 1850', *Journal of Social History,* V (Fall, 1971), 71-96.

Moll-Weiss, Augusta, *Les écoles ménagères à l'étranger et en France,* Paris, 1908.

Moll-Weiss, Augusta, *Les gens de maison,* Paris, 1927.

Mouillon, Marthe-Juliette, 'Un exemple de migration rurale: de la Somme dans la capitale. Domestique de la Belle Epoque à Paris (1904-1912)', *Études de la Région parisienne,* XLIV (July, 1970), 1-9.

Munby, A.J.M., *Faithful Servants,* London, 1891.

Murray, Ross, *The Modern Householder: A Manual of Domestic Economy in all its Branches,* London, 1872.

Murray, Ross, ed., *Warne's Model Housekeeper: A Manual of Domestic Economy,* London [1873].

Neff, Wanda, F., *Victorian Working Women,* New York, 1929.

Nelham, Thomas A., *The Workmen's Compensation Act, 1906,* London, 1907.

New System of Practical Domestic Economy, A., 3rd ed., London, 1823.

Nord, Départment du, *Rapport sur l'enseignement ménager,* Lille, 1909.

Noriac, Jules, *Les gens de Paris,* Paris, 1867.

Office du Travail, Ministère du Commerce et de l'Industrie, *Enquête sur le placement des employés, ouvriers et domestiques à Paris, depuis la promulgation de la loi du 14 mars 1904,* Paris, 1909.

Office du Travail, *Le placement des employés, ouvriers et domestiques en France, son histoire, son état actuel,* Paris, 1893.

Office du Travail, *Seconde Enquête sur le placement des employés, des ouvriers, et des domestiques,* Paris, 1901.

Oliver, L., *Domestic Servants and Citizenship,* London, 1911.

Oram, G., *Masters and Servants,* London, 1858.

Panton, Mrs J.E., *From Kitchen to Garret. Hints for Young Householders,* London, 1890.

Panton, Mrs J.E., *Homes of Taste. Economical Hints,* London, 1890.

Panton, Mrs J.E., *Leaves from a Housekeeper's Book,* London, 1914.

Parent-Duchâtelet, Dr Alexandre, *De la prostitution dans la ville de Paris,* 2 vols., Paris, 1836.

Paris, *Recherches statistiques sur la ville de Paris et le départment de la Seine,* 6 vols. Paris, 1821-1860.

Pariset, Madame, *Manuel de la maîtresse de la maison, ou lettres sur*

131

l'économie domestique, Paris, 1821.

Parkes, Mrs William, *Domestic Duties or Instructions to Young Married Ladies on the Management of their Households,* London, 1825.

Parkyn, E.A., *The Law of Master and Servant,* London, 1897.

Paroisse bretonne, La, Monthly, 1914-1921.

Paterson, J., *Notes on the Law of Master and Servant,* London, 1897.

Pedly, Mrs, *Infant Nursing and the Management of Young Children,* London, 1866.

Pellarin, Charles, 'Maître et servante', *L'Avenir des Femmes,* IX (1877), 183.

Perennes, François, *La domesticité avant et depuis 1789,* Paris, 1844.

Perkin, Harold J., *The Origins of Modern English Society, 1780-1880,* London, 1969.

Perrot, Marguerite, *Le Mode de Vie des Familles Bourgeoises,* Paris, 1961.

Personnaz, Andre, *Le louage des domestiques,* Paris, Thèse de droit, 1909.

Peterson, M. Jeanne, 'The Victorian Governess: Status Incongruence in Family and Society', *Suffer and Be Still,* ed. Martha Vicinus, Bloomington, Indiana, 1972.

Philip, R. Kemp, *The Practical Housewife,* London, 1855.

Piffault, A, *La femme du foyer,* Paris, 1908.

Pinchbeck, Ivy, *Women Workers in the Industrial Revolution, 1750-1850,* London, 1930.

Powell, Margaret, *Below Stairs,* London, 1968.

Present for Servants, A. London, 1807.

Quinlan, M. J., *Victorian Prelude: A History of English Manners,* New York, 1941.

Rayner, John, *Employers and their Female Domestics: Their Respective Rights and Responsibilities,* London, 1895.

Redford, Arthur, *Labor Migration in England, 1800-1850,* New York, 1968.

Ribbé, Charles de, *Les domestiques dans la famille,* Paris, 1862.

Richard, Henri, *Du louage des services domestiques en droit français,* Angers, Thèse de droit, 1906.

Richardson, Sheila J., *The Servant Question: A Study of the Domestic Labour Market, 1851-1911,* unpublished thesis, M. Phil., University of London, 1967.

Ris-Paquot, *Le livre de la femme d'intérieur,* Paris, 1891.

Robert, Edmond, *Les domestiques étude de moeurs et d'histoire,* Paris, 1875.

Roue, Paul, *Code domestique. Maîtres et serviteurs. Bureaux de placement,* Paris, 1903.

Routh, Guy, *Occupation and Pay in Great Britain, 1906-1960,*

Cambridge, 1965.

Rowntree, B. Seebhom, *Poverty. A Study of Town Life,* London, 1903.

Royden, A. M. *et al., Downward Paths: An Inquiry into the Causes which Contribute to the Making of Prostitution,* London, 1916.

Ryckère, Raymond de, *La servante criminelle, étude de criminologie professionelle,* Paris, 1908.

Salmon, Lucy Maynard, *Domestic Service,* 2nd ed. New York, 1901.

Salmon, Georges, 'La domesticité', *La Nouvelle Revue,* XXXVIII (1886), 529-567.

Sauty, Robert, *De la condition juridique des domestiques,* Paris, Thèse de droit, 1911.

Schirmacher, Dr Kaethe, 'Le travail domestique des femmes', *Revue d'Économie Politique,* XVIII (1904), 353-379.

Schmahl, Jeanne, 'L'Assistance et l'éducation des jeunes servantes à Paris et à Londres', *Revue philanthropique,* II (1897), 187-195.

Scott, Joan and Louise Tilly, 'Women's Work and the Family in Nineteenth-Century Europe', *The Family in History,* ed. Charles E. Rosenburg, Philadelphia, 1975, pp.18-21.

Servais, Jean-Jacques and Jean-Pierre Laurend, *Histoire et Dossier de la Prostitution,* Paris, 1965.

Servants and Masters, By a Barrister, London, 1892.

Servants' Benevolent Institution, *Report,* London, 1846.

Servants' Institution, The, *An Address from the Managers,* London, 1835.

Servants' Magazine, The, Monthly, 1838-1869.

Servants' Practical Guide, The, London, 1880.

Serviteur, Le, Monthly, 1905-1912.

Shorter, Edward, 'Female Emancipation, Birth Control and Fertility in European History', *American Historical Review,* LXXVII (1973), 605-640.

Shorter, Edward, 'Illegitimacy, Sexual Revolution, and Social Change in Modern Europe', *Journal of Interdisciplinary History,* II, no.2 (Autumn, 1971), 237-272.

Siegfried, Andre, 'Budgets d'hier et d'aujourd'hui', *Le Figaro,* 17 mars 1954.

Simiand, François, *Le Salaire, L'Évolution sociale, et la Monnaie,* 3 vols., Paris, 1932.

Simon, Jules, *L'ouvrière,* 4th ed., Paris, 1862.

Simon, Jules, 'Le travail et le salaire des femmes', *Revue des Deux-Mondes,* February 15, 1860.

Singer-Kérel, Jeanne, *Le Coût de la vie à Paris de 1840 à 1954,* Paris, 1961.

Soboul, Albert, *Les Sans-Culottes Parisiens en l'an II,* Paris, 1958.

Société des Sciences morales, des Lettres, et des Arts de Seine-et-Oise,

Memoirs, 7 vols., Versailles, 1847-1866.

Southgate, H., *Things a Lady Would Like to Know Concerning Domestic Management and Expenditure,* 2nd ed., London, 1875.

Soyer, Alexis, *The Modern Housewife or Ménagère,* American ed., New York, 1860.

Spofford, Harriet Prescott, *The Servant Girl Question,* Boston, 1881.

Statistique générale de la France, Bureau de la, *Statistique de la France, Résultats statistiques du dénombrement de la population,* 1851-1921, Strasbourg, 1855-1869; Paris, 1873-1925.

Statistique générale de la France, Bureau de la, *Album graphique de la Statistique générale,* Paris, 1907.

Statistique générale de la France, Bureau de la, *Annuaire statistique de la France,* 1875-1915, Paris, 1878-1918.

Statistique générale de la France, Bureau de la, *Annuaire statistique de la ville de Paris,* 1880-1911, Paris, 1880-1914.

Statistique générale de la France, Bureau de la, *Bulletin de la Statistique générale de la France,* 4 vols., Paris, 1911-1915.

Statistique générale de la France, Bureau de la, *Prix et salaires à diverses époques,* Strasbourg, 1863.

Statistique générale de la France, Bureau de la, *Salaire et coût de l'éxistence à diverses époques jusqu'en 1910,* Paris, 1911.

Statistique générale de la France, Bureau de la, *Statistique annuelle,* 1871-1900, 27 vols., Paris, 1874-1904.

Statistique générale de la France, Bureau de la, *Statistique des Familles en 1906,* Paris, 1912.

Statistique générale de la France, Bureau de la, *Statistique des Familles et des Habitations en 1911,* Paris, 1918.

Stearns, Peter N., 'Working-Class Women in Britain, 1890-1914', *Suffer and Be Still,* ed. Martha Vicinus, Bloomington, Ind., 1972, pp.100-120.

Stearns, Peter N., *Lives of Labour,* London, 1975.

Stigler, George, *Domestic Servants in the United States, 1900-1940,* New York, National Bureau of Economic Research, Occasional Paper, 1946.

Sue, Eugène, *Martin, l'enfant trouvé ou les mémoirs d'un valet de chambre,* 12 vols., Paris, 1846-1847.

Teale, T.P., *Dangers to Health in our own Houses,* London, 1877.

Théron de Montaugé, Louis, *La crise agricole dans les pays à céréales,* Toulouse, 1875.

Thierry, Dr Henry and Dr Lucien Graux, *L'Habitation urbaine,* Paris, 1909.

Thomas, Edith, *Les Femmes de 1848,* Paris, 1948.

Thomas, Edith, *Les Petroleuses,* Paris, 1963.

Thompson, F.M.L., *English Landed Society in the Nineteenth Century,* London, 1963.

Thuard, Emile, *Du Placement des Ouvriers et Domestiques en France et à l'Etranger*, Les Mans, 1904.

Tilly, Charles and C. Harold Brown, 'On Uprooting, Kinship, and the Auspices of Migration', *International Journal of Comparative Sociology*, VI (1965), 139-164.

Toledano, André Daniel, *La vie de famille sous la restauration et la monarchie de juillet*, Paris, 1943.

Towner, Lawrence W., 'A Fondness for Freedom: Servant Protests in Puritan Society', *William and Mary Quarterly*, XIX, 3rd series (April, 1962), 201-219.

Trégoat, Dr A.G., *L'Émigration bretonne à Paris*, Paris, 1900.

Turner, Ernest Sackville, *What the Butler Saw: 250 Years of the Servant Problem*, London, 1962.

Tytler, Elizabeth, 'The Eternal Servant Problem', *The National Review*, LIII (March-August, 1909), 972-981.

Ulliac-Trémadeure, S. (Mlle), *La maîtresse de maison*, Paris, 1859.

'Veritas, Amara', *The Servant Problem: An Attempt at Its Solution by an Experienced Mistress*, London, 1899.

Vincent, V. (Madame), 'La domesticité féminine', *La Réforme sociale*, II (July-December, 1901, 5th series), 510-519.

Vincent, V. (Madame), 'Rapport sur le travail des bonnes', *Congrès féministe international de 1900*, Paris, 1900.

Walkowitz, Judith R. and Daniel J., 'We are not Beasts of the Field': Prostitution and the Poor in Plymouth and Southampton under the Contagious Diseases Act', *Clio's Consciousness Raised*, eds. Mary S. Hartman and Lois Banner, New York, 1974, pp.192-225.

Walsh, J.H., *A Manual of Domestic Economy Suited to Families Spending from £100 to £1000 a Year*, London, 1857.

Warren, Mrs Eliza, *How I Managed my House on Two Hundred Pounds a Year*, London, 1864.

Webb, Catherine, 'An Unpopular Industry', *Nineteenth Century*, LIII (January-June, 1903), 989-1001.

Webb, Sidney and Beatrice, *Industrial Democracy*, London, 1902.

Weber, A., *Des Usages locaux*, Orleans, 1882.

Weber, Adna, *The Growth of Cities in the Nineteenth Century*, Ithaca, N.Y., 1963.

Webster, Thomas and Mrs Parkes, *An Encyclopedia of Domestic Economy*, London, 1844.

Why do Servants of the Nineteenth Century Dress as They Do? 2nd ed., London, 1859.

Wood, George, 'The Course of Women's Wages During the Nineteenth Century', *A History of Factory Legislation*, eds. B. L. Hutchins and A. Harrison, Westminster, 1903, pp.257-316.

Wood, G.H., 'Real Wages and the Standard of Comfort Since 1850',
Journal of the Royal Statistical Society, LXXII (March, 1909),
91-103.

Wright, Lawrence, *Clean and Decent: The Fascinating History of the
Bathroom and the W.C.,* London, 1960.

Wright, Lawrence, *Homes Fires Burning: The History of Domestic
Heating and Cooking,* London, 1964.

Yvernès, Émile, 'La criminalité et le dénombrement (1861-1891)',
Journal de la Société de Statistique de Paris, XXXVI (1895),
314-325.

Zeldin, Theodore, *France, 1848-1945,* vol. I, Oxford, 1973.

Zola, Émile, *Pot-Bouille,* Paris, 1928.

Family Papers

A. N., 27A.P. 17, dossier 3, Papiers de François de Neufchâteau,
Carnets de comptes, 1815-1827.

A.N., 82A.P. 8, dossier 3, Papiers de la générale Laure Bro de Coméres,
1829-1844.

A.N., 82 A.P. 10, Agendas et Carnets de comptes de M. le Baron Olivier
Bro de Comères.

A.N., 93 A.P. 2, Livres de comptes de Madame Veuve Joré, 1828-1836.

A. N., 107 A.P. 18, dossier 2, Livre de comptes, environ 1774 (famille
Galliffet).

A. N., 107 A. P. 18, dossier 6, Livre de comptes de Justin de Galliffet
et de sa femme, 1810-1812.

A. N., 107 A. P. 18, dossier 7, Livre de comptes commencé en 1822.

A. N., 111 A. P. 74, dossier 3, Papiers de la famille de Beaumont, Livre
de comptes de Christophe-François, marquis de Beaumont,
1848-1851.

A. N., 111 A. P. 77, dossier 2, Carnets de comptes de Eliacin de
Beaumont, 1851-1882.

A. N., 112 A. P. 2, dossier 3, Papiers du Baron de Senegra,
Administration de la maison de Louis Bonaparte, roi de Hollande
par Senegra, 1800-1807.

A. N., 133 A. P. 2, dossier 5, Dépenses de la maison de Maréchal
Davout pendant 1809, 1810.

A. N., 133 A. P. 3, dossier 4, Note sur les domestiques de M. le
Gouverneur à Brieuc.

A. N., 140 A. P. 5, dossier 1, Projet d'un bureau de placement,
1816-1817.

A. N., 140 A. P. 11, dossier 1, Comptes divers de Camille Jubé de la
Perrelle.

A. N., 154 A. P. V 41 (microfilm, 177 mi 308), Comptes de la maison
de M. le Comte de Nantouillet, 1815-1823.

A. N., 272 A. P. 26, dossier 4, Comptes de Madame Veuve de Ploeuc,

1870-1875.

A. N., 272 A. P. 27, Livre de raison de Jerome d'Hervé, 1879.

A. D. de l'Ardèche, J 303, Livre de raison de Barthelémy Riou, 1812-1849.

A. D. des Ardennes, 2 J 77 (10), Journaux des dépenses du ménage de Madame veuve Vermon, 1826-1838 (3 registres).

A. D. des Ardennes, 2 J 77 (11), Journaux des dépenses du ménage de Docteur Crequy, 1826-1868 (25 registres).

A. D. des Landes, 1 F 968, Livre de raison de Pierre-Chevalier Blondiet, 1812-1872.

A. D. de Loire-Atlantique, 3 J 26, Registre de dépenses domestiques (d'origine inconnue, région de Pontchateau), 1818-1828.

A. D. de Loire-Atlantique, 11 J 1, Livre pour servier à mettre les décharges (papiers Pichelin), 1718-1933.

A. D. du Puy-de-Dôme, J 799, Livres de comptes, 1843-1844 (2 registres).

A. D. du Puy-de-Dôme, J 924-925, Livres de comptes, 1828-1849 (2 registres).

Official Documents

A. N., AF IV 484, plaquet 3700, Rapport du duc de Rovigo, Savary, à l'Empereur sur le placement des domestiques.

A. N., 88 AQ 1-6, Caisse d'Épargne et de Prévoyance à Paris, Rapports et Comptes-Rendus, présentés à l'Assemblée générale, 1810-1915.

A. N., BB ^{30} 373, Rapport du procureur-général de Haute-Saône, Besançon, 9 avril 1859.

A. N., BB ^{30} 493, Projet de loi sur l'abrogation de l'article 1781 du code Napoleon relatif au louage des domestiques et ouvriers (1868), Corps legislatif, Session 1868, no. 173.

A. N., C 1127, dossier 121, L'abrogation de l'article 1781 du code Napoleon, 27 juillet 1868.

A. N., C 2868, dossier 726, Proposition de loi portant établissement d'une taxe sur les domestiques, 26 juin 1872, Assemblée nationale, no. 1247.

A. N., F ^{7} 9817, dossier on the placement of workers and domestics kept by the police.

A. N., F ^{7} 13718, dossier 2, police file on Congrès national des gens de maison, le 21-25 mai 1909, Paris.

A. N., F ^{20} 724, Livrets des Caisses d'Épargne, 1835-1839.

A. N., F ^{22} 367, Plaintes relatives à l'inobservation du repos hebdomadaire (1899-1920 environ), dossier 'domestiques'.

Vital Records

London. Census of England and Wales, 1851 and 1871. Manuscript enumeration lists.

Lyon. Listes nominatives du dénombrement de la population, 1872-1876, A. D. du Rhône, Série M.

Paris. Déclarations des Mutations par Décès à Paris, D. Q.[7] 3417-3939 (1825), 3532-4022 (1853), 10.611-10.704 (1869), A. D. de Paris.

Versailles. Listes nominatives du dénombrement de la population, 1820-1911, A, D. des Yvelines, 9 M 954.

Versailles. Série E, Registres des Actes de Mariages, 1825-1833 and 1845-1853; Tables des Contrats de Mariages, 1825-March 1834 and 1845-1854.

NOTES

INTRODUCTION

1. There is only one recent historical monograph on servants, J. Jean Hecht, *The Domestic Servant Class in Eighteenth-Century England* (London, 1956). French historian and demographer Abel Chatelain outlined the significance of domestic service for feminine urban migration in 'Migrations et domesticité féminine urbaine en France, XVIIIe - XXe siècles', *Revue historique économique et sociale* (1969, no. 4), pp. 506-528. Recent work on domestics include Leonore Davidoff, 'Mastered for Life: Servant and Wife in Victorian and Edwardian England', *Journal of Social History*, VII, no. 4 (Summer, 1974), 406-428, and important comparative research by David Chaplin, Department of Sociology, Western Michigan University, whose papers include 'Domestic Service and the Rationalisation of Household Economy, Outline for a Comparative Study' (mimeo) and 'Private Household Employment in the United States', a research paper for the U.S. Department of Labor, 1969.

2. Adeline Daumard, *La Bourgeoisie parisienne* (Paris, 1963), hereinafter cited as Daumard, 1963; Louis Chevalier, *La formation de la population parisienne au XIXe siècle* (Paris, 1950), hereinafter cited as Chevalier, *La formation.*

3. J. A. Banks, *Prosperity and Parenthood* (London, 1954), p.73.

4. J. F. C. Harrison, *The Early Victorians, 1832-1851* (London, 1971), p.46.

5. *Ibid,* p.110.

6. Abel Chatelain, 'La formation de la population lyonnaise, apports savoyards au XVIIIe siecle', *Revue de géographie de Lyon,* XXVI (1951 no. 3), 345-349.

7. Chevalier, *La formation,* p.40.

8. Censuses were often unclear as to the exact occupation of a domestic servant, and the confounding of categories of agricultural workers and household servants occurs frequently. In addition, some servants moved back and forth between one kind of service and the other so that segregation of the two groups is very difficult. Hence, while the two groups had distinctive characteristics and problems, it is often impossible to discriminate between them, however desirable this may be.

9. Samuel and Sarah Adams, *The Complete Servant* (London, 1825), p.233.

10. G. Oram, *Masters and Servants* (London, 1858), pp.15, 28; Mrs Isabella Beeton, *Beeton's Book of Household Management* (London, 1861), pp.21-24.

11. Louis Alq, *Le maître et la maîtresse de maison* (Paris, 1882, new edit.), p.193; *Les Français peints par eux-mêmes, encyclopédie morale au XIXe siècle* (Paris, 1840-50, 8 vols.), I, p.294, hereinafter cited as 'Les Français'.

12. Remy Dubois, *De la condition juridique des domestiques* (Lille, 1907), p.67; Archives nationales, 107 A. P. 18, dossier 7, papers of the Galliffet family list the costs of their wet nurses.

13. Beeton, p.1020; *The Domestic Service Guide* (London, 1865), pp.227-251.

14. Marcel Cusenier, *Les Domestiques en France* (Paris, 1912), pp.56-58.

15. Wanda F. Neff, *Victorian Working Women* (New York, 1929), p.153; T. Henry Baylis, *Workmen's Compensation Act, 1906* (London, 1907); S. and S. Adams, p.272 and 275; M. Jeanne Peterson, 'The Victorian Governess: Status Incongruence in Family and Society' in *Suffer and Be Still: Women in the Victorian Age,* ed. Martha Vicinus (Bloomington, Ind.: 1972), pp.3-19, *passim.*

139

16. On the 'femme de ménage': *Les Français*, I, p.326; Paul Roué, *Code domestique, Maîtres et Serviteurs, Bureaux de Placement* (Paris, 1903), p.94; on the charwoman: Edward Cadbury *et al.*, *Women's Work and Wages* (London, 1906), p.112; Clementina Black, ed., *Married Women's Work* (London, 1915), p.216; L. Wyatt Papworth, 'Charwomen', *Married Women's Work*, pp.105-113, *passim*.

17. Adeline Daumard, 'Une réference pour l'étude des sociétés urbaines en France au XVIIIᵉ et XIXᵉ siecles, projet de code socio-professionnel', *Revue d'histoire moderne et contemporaine*, X (1963), 201.

18. *Ibid.*, p.192.

19. *Statistique générale*, 1861; see also Chapter 2.

20. *Ibid.*, 1896; see also Chapter 2.

21. *Ibid.*, 1886, p.149.

22. Adeline Daumard, *La Bourgeoisie parisienne* (Paris, 1970, abr.), p.21, used this percentage to define the limits of the middle class, but this method is unreliable: see Chapter 1.

23. *Statistique générale*, 1901, IV, 41 and 511.

24. Census of England and Wales, 1861, P.P., 1863, LIII, Pt.1, p.18.

25. Census of England and Wales, 1861 to 1921. The 1891 census may not be reliable on the number of servants, since the census category was changed to include some women who helped with the housework in their family home.

26. David Chaplin, 'Domestic Service as a Family Activity and as an Occupation during Industrialisation', paper presented at the International Sociological Association, Bulgaria, 1970, p.1; see also Margo L. Smith, 'Domestic Service as a Channel of Upward Mobility for the Lower-Class Woman: the Lima Case', in Ann Pescatello, ed., *Female and Male in Latin America* (Pittsburgh: 1973), pp.192-207

27. Esther Boserup, *Women's Role in Economic Development* (London, 1970), p.102-104.

28. Georges Rudé, *The Crowd in the French Revolution* (Oxford, 1959), p.65; P.-J.-B. Buchez and P.-C. Roux, *Histoire parlementaire de la Révolution française*, 2 vols. (Paris, 1834), II, p.359.

29. Pierre Jouhaud, *Paris dans le dix-neuvième siècle ou Réflexions d'un observateur.* . . (Paris, 1809), p.293.

30. Constitution of the Year III, Title II, article 13; Constitution of the Year VIII, Title I, article 5: Leon Hom, *De la situation juridique des gens de service* (Paris, 1901), p.93.

31. L. Oliver, *Domestic Servants and Citizenship* (London, 1911), *passim;* Emile Corra, *La Domesticité* (Paris, 1908), p.23: servants are 'so closely associated with the vicissitudes of our intimate life that one could never completely assimilate them into ordinary salaried workers.'

32. Marius-Henri-Casimir Mittre, *Des Domestiques en France, dans leur rapports avec l'économie sociale, le bonheur domestique, les lois civiles, criminelles, et de police* (Paris, 1838), p.7; also see Chapter 2.

33. Chevalier, *La formation*, p.40.

34. Madame Pariset, *Manuel de la Maîtresse de la Maison ou Lettres sur l'Economie domestique* (Paris, 1821).

35. *A New System of Practical Domestic Economy*, 3rd ed. (London, 1823); Samuel and Sarah Adams, *The Complete Servant* (London, 1825), and Mrs William Parkes, *Domestic Duties or Instructions to Young Married Ladies on the Management of their Households* (London, 1825) were among the earliest English manuals.

36. Peter N. Stearns, 'Working-Class Women in Britain, 1890-1914,' *Suffer and Be Still: Women in the Victorian Age*, ed. Martha Vicinus (Bloomington, Ind., 1972), p.110; see Chapter 7 for a fuller discussion of this decline.

37. Frédéric Le Play, *La Réforme sociale en France,* 2 vols. (Paris, 1864),
     I, p.227.
38. Rosamond Bayne-Powell, *Housekeeping in the Eighteenth Century*
     (London, 1956), p.141; Georgiana Hill, *Women in English Life from
     Medieval to Modern Times,* 2 vols. (London, 1896), II, p.210; Mrs Parkes,
     p.131.

CHAPTER 1

1.   Adeline Daumard, *Les Bourgeois de Paris au XIXe siècle,* Paris, 1970.
2.   Banks, pp. 70-71.
3.   Marion Lochhead, *The Victorian Household* (London, 1964), p.30.
4.   Quoted in Sheila Richardson's, 'The Servant Question: A Study of the
     Domestic Labour Market, 1851-1911', unpublished master's thesis in
     Sociology, 1971, University of London, p.35.
5.   Chevalier, *La formation,* p.79.
6.   Lyon, Listes nominatives du dénombrement de 1872, A. D., Rhône,
     Série M, XI-XXIII.
7.   Adeline Daumard, *La Bourgeoisie parisienne de 1815 à 1848,* Paris, 1963.
8.   *Ibid.,* p.403.
9.   Geoffrey Best, *Mid-Victorian Britain, 1851-1875* (New York, 1972),
     pp.82-83. Note that income tax figures exclude middle-class individuals
     whose incomes were between £100 and £200.
10. See Chapter 2.
11. Albert Babeau, *Les artisans et les domestiques d'autrefois* (Paris, 1886),
     p.291.
12. Alq, p.183.
13. *The Book of Domestic Duties* (London, 1835), p.16; see similar statement
     in Pariset, p.162.
14. For example, H. de Gallier, 'Comment on était servi autrefois', *La Revue,*
     LXXXVI (June 15, 1910), 491-492; see also Hecht, p.5.
15. A. N., 154 A. P. V 41 (Fonds Tocqueville), household accounts from 1815
     to 1827.
16. F. M. L. Thompson, *English Landed Society in the Nineteenth Century*
     (London, 1963), p.95.
17. Versailles, Listes nominatives du dénombrement de 1872, A. D., Yvelines
     9 M 954 ^{12}.
18. Lyon, Listes nominatives, 1872.
19. Alq, p.163.
20. Banks, p.134.
21. Banks, p.71; Mrs J. E. Panton insisted that a young couple starting out
     could manage with only two maids and a man to help out, *Leaves from a
     Housekeeper's Book* (London, 1914), p.55.
22. *Economy for the Single and Married* (London, [1845]), p.25.
23. Mrs Beeton, p.8; S. and S. Adams, p.5; *A New System,* p.37; Thomas
     Webster and Mrs Parkes, *An Encyclopedia of Domestic Economy*
     (London, 1844), p.331; Mrs Eliza Warren, *How I Managed My House on
     Two Hundred Pounds a Year* (London, 1864), p.12.
24. Beeton, p.8; *A New System,* p.39; Webster, p.331.
25. For an excellent discussion of middle-class incomes see Patricia Branca,
     Silent Sisterhood: Middle-Class Women in the Victorian Home (London,
     1975), Chapter Three.
26. Charles Booth, *Life and Labour of the People of London* (London, 1903),
     VIII, p.221.
27. These figures are drawn from random samples of the manuscript census

lists of London in 1851 and 1871.

28. The liberal professions in France constituted 1.4 per cent of the total population while employing 2.8 per cent of the total number of servants. *Statistique générale,* 1872, p.xxxi.

29. Paris, *Recherches statistiques sur la ville de Paris et le départment de la Seine* (under the direction of Prefect Haussmann), VI (Paris, 1860), pp.648-649.

30. *Statistique générale,* 1872, pp.254-255.

31. These percentages should of course be considered in terms of the age structure of the professional population but this information is unavailable. It is possible that young professionals who did not employ a servant when starting their careers could expect in their mature years to afford domestic help. Nevertheless, the great disparity between the total number of professionals in particular groups and the total number of servants employed remains convincing evidence that many professionals never employed a live-in servant. In the study by Marguerite Perrot of 327 family budgets for the period from 1873 to 1913, all of the families kept at least one servant. But the segments of the middle classes who were most likely to employ only one servant or none at all were either missing or underrepresented in the study. Marguerite Perrot, *Le mode de vie des familles bourgeoises* (Paris, 1961), *passim.*

32. Louis Chevalier, *Classes laborieuses et classes dangereuses à Paris pendant la première moitié du XIXe siècle* (Paris, 1958).

33. *Ibid.,* p.71.

34. *Ibid.,* p.553.

35. Alexandre-Jean-Baptiste Parent-Duchatelet, *De la prostitution dans la ville de Paris,* 2 vols. (Paris, 1836); Henry Mayhew, *London Labour and the London Poor* (London, 1861; reprinted New York, 1968), VI; Booth, VIII.

36. B. H. de Paris, 131489, Décret imperial, 3 octobre, 1810.

37. A. N., 140 A. P. 5, dossier 1, letter of Passart.

38. Jouhaud, p.293.

39. On the applicability of Chevalier's thesis for the lower classes generally, see the review of Chevalier's book by Robert J. Bezucha, *Journal of Social History,* vol.VIII, no.1 (Fall, 1974), 119-124.

40. Sarah Stickney Ellis, *The Women of England,* 2nd ed. (London, 1839). p.304. Factory managers had a similar opportunity but they constituted a much smaller percentage of the middle classes than the whole group of servant-employers.

41. Mittre, p.146.

42. A. de Doncourt, *Guerre aux Petits Abus domestiques: L'Anse du Panier* (Paris, n.d.), p.26.

43. Alq, p.150.

44. Beeton, pp. 6-9.

45. Pariset, p.187.·

46. Lady Marie Willoughby de Broke, 'The Pros and Cons of Domestic Service,' *The National Review,* LX (September-February, 1913), 453.

47. Warren, *How I Managed,* preface; Lady A. S. Baker, *Our Responsibilities and Difficulties as Mistresses of Young Servants* (London, 1886), p.6.

48. *La Fronde,* September 7, 1900.

49. *Ibid.*

50. Bouniceau-Gesmon, *Domestiques et Maîtres* (Paris, 1896), p.168.

51. Mittre, p.181; J. H. Walsh, *A Manual of Domestic Economy* (London, 1857), pp.224-225.

52. E. A. Parkyn, *The Law of Master and Servant* (London, 1897), p.51; Comtesse de Genlis, *Le 'La Bruyère' des domestiques précédé de considérations sur l'état de domesticité en général* (Paris, 1828), pp.163-166.

53. Guillaume-Louis-Gustave Belèze, *Le Livre des Ménages: nouveau manuel d'économie domestique* (Paris, 1861), p.366: an English servant wrote that servants should be treated as intelligent human beings in order to win their respect and loyalty, Nellie Anderson, 'A Servant's View of the Servant Problem,' *The National Review*, LXI (March-August, 1913), 124.
54. Mittre, p.231.
55. Elizabeth Bayle-Mouillard (Madame Celnart), *Manuel complet des domestiques, ou l'art de former de bons servituers* (Paris, 1836), p.175, hereinafter cited as Celnart.
56. *Lady Servants – For and Against* (London, 1906), p.4 .
57. *Book of Domestic Duties*, pp.18-19.
58. Octave, Mirbeau, *Le Journal d'une femme de chambre* (Paris, 1900), p.401.
59. William Johnson, *The Servant Problem. Can It Be Solved? Why Not?* (London, 1922), pp.8-9.
60. Pariset, p.24.
61. *Ibid.*, p.173.
62. Celnart, p.176.
63. E. Dufaux de la Jonchère, *Ce que les maîtres et les domestiques doivent savoir* (Paris, 1884), pp.365-366.
64. Maurice Beaufreton, 'Comment se resoudra la question des domestiques', *La Quinzaine,* LXXII (1906), 549.
65. Cusenier, p.180.
66. Davidoff, p.412.
67. Clementina Black, 'The Dislike to Domestic Service', *Nineteenth Century,* XXXVIII (January-June, 1893), 454.
68. Celnart, pp.11-12; Ris-Paquot, *Le livre de la femme d'intérieur* (Paris, 1891), p.39; *Domestiques d'aujourd'hui* (Paris, 1877), p.18.
69. *Why Do Servants of the Nineteenth Century Dress as They do?* 2nd ed., (London, 1859), p.viii; Parkes, p.122; Webster, p.328.
70. Dufaux, p.95.
71. Marie Delorme, 'Les domestiques,' *L'Enseignement ménager* (November, 1906), p.197; similarly in Baylis, p.35.
72. Dufaux, p.322.
73. Lucien Haas and Eugène Penancier, *Maîtres et Gens de Service* (Paris, 1925), p.185-186.
74. *Ibid.*
75. *Servants and Masters. The Law of Disputes, Rights, and Remedies in Plain Language. By a Barrister* (London, 1892), p.14.
76. Parkyn, p.51.
77. Dufaux, p.77; *Journal des Gens de Maison,* January 8, 1894; Baylis, pp.12-17; Walsh, p.224; T. G. Mann, *The Duties of an Experienced Servant* (London, 1894), pp.29-31.
78. Walsh, *op.cit,* John Rayner, *Employers and Their Female Domestics: Their Respective Rights and Responsibilities* (London, 1895), p.49.
79. Walsh, p.225.
80. Alfred Franklin, *La vie privée d'autrefois,* 27 vols. (Paris, 1887-1902), XX, p.59.
81. Statistique générale de la France, *Annuaire statistique de la France,* 1886, p.186.
82. B. L. Hutchins, *Statistics of Women's Life and Employment* (London, 1909, reprinted from the *Journal of the Royal Statistical Society*), p.26.
83. *British Medical Journal,* June 19, 1869.
84. See Chapter 3.
85. See Chapter 6.
86. Madame Guizot, *Education domestique,* 2 vols, 6th ed. (Paris, 1881), I, p.309.

87.   Mrs Eliot James, *Our Servants: Their Duties to Us and Ours to Them* (London, 1883), p.76.

88.   Daumard, 1970, p.190ff; Best, pp.278-281.

89.   Olivier Fourcade, *De la condition civile des domestiques* (Paris, Thèse de Droit, 1901), pp.16-17; Parkyn, p.9; Rayner, p.32; *The Servant's Practical Guide* (London, 1880), p.11; J. Paterson, *Notes on the Law of Master and Servant* (London, 1897), p.15.

90.   Ellis, p.242; similarly in Alq, p.3.

91.   Spofford, *The Servant Girl Question* (Boston, 1881), p.100.

92.   Pariset, p.3; similarly in *The Hand-Book of Women's Work* (London, 1876), pp.6-7.

93.   'Justice,' *Solution of the Domestic Servant Problem. How to Get the Right Kind of Girl into Domestic Service* (North Shields, 1910), *passim.*

94.   Delorme, p.229; Cusenier, pp.172-174; Madame Vincent, *Rapport sur le Travail des Bonnes, Congrès feministes internationaux de 1900* (Paris, 1900), p.t.

95.   Mademoiselle Châtenay, *Rapports sur l'Enseignement Ménager et les Écoles Ménagères* (Angers, 1909), p.6.

96.   Department du Nord, *Rapport sur l'Enseignement Ménager* (Lille, 1909), p.4.

97.   Josephine Kamm, *Hope Deferred. Girls' Education in English History* (London, 1965), pp.163-164; Helen Campbell, *Women Wage-Workers, Their Trades and Their Lives* (Boston, 1887), p.238; Margaret Hewitt, *Wives and Mothers ménagères a l'Etranger et en France* (Paris, 1908), *passim*; Jeanne E. Schmahl, 'L'Assistance et l'éducation des jeunes servantes à Paris et à Londres', *Revue philanthropique*, II (1897), 187.

98.   Alq, p.130.

99.   Pariset, p.65.

100.   Maurice Allem, *La Vie quotidienne sous le Second Empire* (Paris, 1948), p.117; Mirbeau, p.87.

101.   Beeton, sections 23 and 24.

102.   *Ibid.*

103.   See a similar discussion of this phenomenon in Leonore Davidoff, *The Best Circles* (London, 1973), pp.34-35.

104.   John Burnett, ed., *The Annals of Labour: Autobiographies of British Working Class People, 1820-1920* (Bloomington, Ind., 1974), p.222.

105.   Nellie Anderson, p.126; *Lady Servants,* p.2; Butler, pp.51-53.

106.   Pariset, p.70.

107.   David Chaplin, 'Domestic Service and the Rationalisation of Household Economy, Outline for a Comparative Study', draft of a paper, November, 1968, p.11.

108.   Nellie Anderson, p.124; 'Amara Veritas,' *The Servant Problem: An Attempt at its Solution by an Experienced Mistress* (London, 1899), p.13.

109.   Bouniceau-Gesmon, p.143; Charles de Ribbé, *Les Domestiques dans la famille* (Paris, 1862), p.12.

110.   *Lady Servants,* p.12.

111.   Hill, II, p.210; Corra, p.23.

112.   Gustave Flaubert, *Madame Bovary* (Paris, 1862), pp.181-182.

113.   Société des Sciences Morales, des Lettres, et des Arts de la département de Seine-et-Oise, *Mémoirs*, VIII (1868), ccxiv-ccxvi.

114.   Académie française, Institut de France, 'Discours sur les *prix de vertu*,' *Séances publiques annuelles*, 1886, p.81.

115.   *Ibid.*, 1875, p.78.

116.   Paris, A. D. de Paris, D. Q. [7] 3532-4022, Déclarations des mutations par décès, 1853.

117.   *Ibid.*, testament of Marie Arthuad, April 4, 1853.

144

118. *Lady Servants,* p.12.
119. Butler, p.34.
120. Alq, p.154.
121. Marthe-Juliette Mouillon, 'Un exemple de migration rurale: de la Somme dans la capitale. Domestique de la Belle Epoque à Paris (1904-1912),' *Etudes de la Région parisienne,* XLIV (July, 1970), 7.

CHAPTER 2

1. The data for the first half of the century is contained in the *Recherches statistiques sur la ville de Paris et le département de la Seine;* for the second half from the *Statistique générale de la France.*
2. *Census of England and Wales, 1901,* P.P., 1904, CVIII, 83.
3. Adna Weber, *The Growth of Cities in the Nineteenth Century* (New York, 1963), p.77.
4. Butler, p.73; *Lady Servants,* p.17; Hill, II, p.223. See Fig.5.1 in Chapter 5.
5. A. D. des Yvelines, Listes nominatives du dénombrement de la population, 1820, 9 M 954 2-3.
6. *Ibid.,* 1872.
7. Daumard, p.227.
8. *Census of England and Wales,* 1851 and 1871; random samples of the manuscript census lists for London.
9. *Statistique générale de la France,* 1901, IV, 509-511.
10. *Ibid.; Census of England and Wales,* III, 24.
11. Butler, p.73; James, p.14.
12. Rowntree, p.391.
13. Booth analysed London's servant class in terms of three groups; the lowest group were daughters of urban labourers or had come from workhouse schools. Booth, IV, pp.213-215.
14. Gareth Stedman Jones in *Outcast London* (London, 1971), p.138, argues that the reason for the high percentage of rural-born individuals in the wealthiest districts of London is the great number of servants in those areas.
15. Olwen Hufton, *The Poor of Eighteenth-Century France, 1750-1789* (Oxford, 1974), p.28.
16. Hecht, pp.16-19; Pinchbeck, p.80.
17. Peter Laslett, *The World We Have Lost* (New York, 1966); Lutz K. Berkner, 'The Stem Family and the Developmental Cycle of the Peasant Household: An Eighteenth-Century Austrian Example', *American Historical Review,* LXXVII (April, 1972), 398-418.
18. See discussion of this aspect of domestic service in Chapter 5.
19. See Tables 5.2, 5.3 and 5.4 in Chapter 5.
20. Hufton, p.28.
21. Marthe-Juliette Mouillon, 'Un exemple de migration rurale de la Somme dans la capitale. Domestique de la Belle Époque', *Etudes de la Région parisienne,* XLIV (July, 1970), 3-4.
22. See John Modell, 'The Peopling of a Working-Class Ward: Reading, Pennsylvania, 1850,' *Journal of Social History,* V, no.1 (1971), 71-96; also see David Chaplin, 'Domestic Service as a Family Activity and as an Occupation During Industrialisation', paper presented to the International Sociological Association, Varna, Bulgaria, September, 1970.
23. Birth rates by department are given in the *Statistique annuelle de la France.*
24. J. C. Goeury, 'Évolution démographique et sociale du faubourg Saint-Germain,' *Contributions à l'Histoire démographique de la Révolution*

française, 2nd series, (Paris 1965), p.53; F. Rousseau-Vigneron, 'La Section de la Place des Fédérés pendant la Révolution,' *Contributions à l'Histoire démographique de la Révolution française,* 3rd series (Paris, 1970), p.168; Martine Sévegrand, 'La Section de Popincourt pendant la Révolution française,' *Contributions à l'Histoire démographique de la Révolution française,* 3rd series (Paris, 1970, p.30).

25. Esther Boserup, *Women's Role in Economic Development* (New York, 1970), pp.102-104.
26. *Ibid.;* Chaplin, 'Domestic Service . . . during Industrialisation', pp.1-3.
27. See discussion of servants' wages in Chapter 3.
28. Abel Chatelain, 'La formation de la population lyonnaise, apports savoyards au XVIIIᵉ siècle', *Revue de Géographie de Lyon,* XXVI, no.3 (1951), 346.
29. See Chapter 4.
30. See note 2, Chapter 4.
31. Weber, p.283.
32. Arthur Redford, *Labor Migration in England, 1800-1850,* revised ed. (New York, 1968), p.183.
33. Weber, p.184.
34. François Simiand, *Le Salaire, L'Évolution sociale, et la Monnaie,* 3 vols. (Paris, 1932), III, tables I and II.
35. Campbell, pp.226-228; Edward Cadbury, *Women's Work and Wages. A Phase of Life in an Industrial City* (London, 1906), pp. 111, 112, and 115; Neff, p.54; Hewitt, p.49.
36. Cadbury, p.115; Black, 'Dislike to Service', p.456.
37. Butler, pp.119-120.
38. *Ibid.*

CHAPTER 3

1. Burnett, p.185.
2. Chatelain, 'Migrations et domesticité', p.508.
3. Webster, p.331; Warren, p.12; Beeton, p.8; S. and S. Adams, p.5.
4. *Economy for the Single and Married,* p.43; Walsh, p.219.
5. *A New System of Practical Domestic Economy,* p.49; Walsh, p.606.
6. Lyon, Archives municipales de Lyon, Recensements fiscaux, 1820, 2ᵉ arrondissement.
7. *Ibid.;* separate rooms for servants in the same building as the employer's apartment may have been less expensive as part of the arrangement for the rental of the employer's own apartment.
8. Perrot, p.81; Singer-Kérel, p.422.
9. Madeleine Auger, *Condition juridique et économique du personnel domestique féminin* (Paris, 1935), p.48.
10. R. Kemp Philip, *The Practical Housewife* (London, 1855); Mrs J. E. Panton, *Leaves from a Housekeeper's Book* (London, 1914), p.24.
11. Rowntree, p.84.
12. Robert Sauty, *De la condition juridique des domestiques* (Paris, 1911), pp.113-114.
13. Panton, *Leaves,* p.99.
14. Cretté-Breton, p.106.
15. *Ibid.,* p.31.
16. Dr Henry Thierry and Dr Lucien Graux, *L'Habitation urbaine* (Paris, 1901), p.7; Commission des logements insalubres de Paris, *Rapport général sur les Travaux de la Commission pendant les années 1862-1865,* A. N., F⁸ 211, p.15.

146

17. 'Consumption and Domestic Service: The Responsibility of Mistresses by a Medical Man', *The Daily Mail,* October 4, 1905, p.9.
18. Dr Paul Juillerat, *L'Hygiène du logement* (Paris, 1909), p.154.
19. A. N. F^{22} 367, letter dated November 18, 1913.
20. Cusenier, p.87.
21. A. Pol., B ^{a} 83.
22. Butler, p.18; Thierry and Graux, p.11; Émile Massard, 'Proposition relative à l'hygiène des habitations de Paris en général et en particulier des logements de concierges, gens de maison, et employés logés', *Conseil municipal de Paris, Rapports* (1909, no.96), p.5; Dr Fernard Barbary, *Semeurs de Bacilles insoupçonnes; Domestiques en service et atteints de tuberculose à forme torpide* (Nice, 1913), p.9.
23. Lyon, Recensements fiscaux, 1820, 2e arrondissement.
24. Massard, no. 96, p.5.
25. Lawrence, Wright, *Home Fires Burning: The History of Domestic Heating and Cooking* (London, 1964), p.121.
26. Thierry and Graux, pp.23-24; *Lady Servants,* p.2.
27. *Ibid.,* p.25; T.P. Teale, *Dangers to Health in Your Own Houses* (London, 1877), *passim.*
28. Juillerat, p.156.
29. Dr Lowenthal, 'État sanitaire et démographie comparée des villes de Paris et de Berlin', *Journal de la Société de Statistique de Paris,* XLVII (1906), p.273; *Lady Servants,* p.2.
30. Dr A.G. Tregoat, *L'Émigration Bretonne à Paris* (Paris, 1900), p.41.
31. 'Consumption and Domestic Service', p.9.
32. Commission des logements insalubres de Paris, *Rapport général sur les travaux de la commission pendant les années 1862-1865* (Paris, 1866), p.15.
33. Ross Murray, ed., *Warne's Model Housekeeper. A Manual of Domestic Economy* (London, 1873), p.26.
34. *The Daily Mail, loc. cit.*
35. Thierry and Graux, p.8.
36. Charles Guillard, 'Rapport présenté au nom de la 6e commission', *Conseil municipal de Paris, Rapports* (1912, no.23), p.4.
37. Massard, no.96, p.12.
38. *Bulletin des ligues sociales d'acheteurs* (2nd trim., 1905), pp.81-82.
39. Butler, p.125ff.
40. Lawrence, Wright, *Clean and Decent* (London, 1960), p.258.
41. Daubié, p.121.
42. Pariset, pp.156-158.
43. Beleze, p.367; Édouard, p.12.
44. *Lady Servants,* p.4; Alq, p.149.
45. Alq, p.150.
46. Booth, VIII, p.219.
47. *How to Improve the Conditions of Domestic Service,* p.13.
48. Letter of Mlle Marie, A.N., F ^{22} 367.
49. S. and S. Adams, p.286.
50. See letter of complaint by a servant named Forestier to *Le Serviteur,* November, 1906.
51. V. Vincent, 'La Domesticité féminine', *La Réforme sociale,* 5th series (July-December, 1901), II, 511; *Lady Servants,* p.2; Butler, pp.51-53.
52. *Le Serviteur,* March, 1906.
53. Campbell, pp.239-240.
54. Butler, pp.51-53.
55. Letters of Madame Alavoine and of the Secretary of 'L'Abeille', A.N., F ^{22} 367.

56. Collet, p.30.
57. A. N., F 22 367, letter of Madame Sayant.
58. *Ibid.*, letter of Eugénie Pinson.
59. *Ibid.*, letter of Madame Gagnepain.
60. Burnett, p.185.
61. Delorem, pp.179-180; Alq, p.141; Pariset, p.78; *Book of Domestic Duties*, pp.18-19; Butler, p.22; Lady A.S. Baker, *Our Responsibilities and Difficulties as Mistresses of Young Servants* (London, 1886), p.8.
62. *Le Serviteur*, February, 1906; Letter of Mlle Marie, A.N., F 22 367; Jules Simon, 'Le Travail et le Salaire des Femmes', *Revue des Deux Mondes* (February 15, 1860), p.918.
63. A. N., 27 A. P. 17, dossier 3; see 1827 in the accounts of François de Neufchâteau.
64. Babeau, p.305.
65. Hecht, pp.158-159.
66. *Ibid.*, pp.163-164.
67. Miss C. Collet, 'Report on Money Wages of In-Door Domestic Servants', P.P., 1899, XCII, C. 9346, 29; Parkes, p.126; Rayner, p.58; *A New System of Practical Domestic Economy*, p.355.
68. Hecht, p.168.
69. A.N., 27A. P. 17, dossier 3.
70. A.D. des Ardennes, 2 J 77 (11), see entries for 1838.
71. A.D. des Ardennes, 2 J 77 (10), see entries for 1836.
72. *The Servant's Practical Guide. A Handbook of Duties and Rules* (London, 1880), p.169.
73. A.N., 272 A. P. 26, dossier 4, see entries for 1871.
74. René Lafabrégue, 'Des enfants trouvés à Paris', *Annales de démographie internationale*, II (1878), 243.
75. Madame Pariset noted this changing practice in regard to the wine allowance as early as 1821, p.108.
76. Baylis, p. 8; Mrs Eliza Warren, *Cookery for Maids of all Work* (London, 1856), pp. x-xi; *The Servant's Practical Guide*, p.164.
77. Booth mentions an average of one pint of beer per day for female servants or the equivalent in money. Booth, VIII, p.220. Similar estimate is found in Parkes, p.117.
78. A. D. des Ardennes, 2 J 77 (10).
79. A. D. du Puy-de-Dôme, J 799.
80. A. N., 272 A. P. 26, dossier 4.
81. Alq, p.211; Jollivet, p.459; account book for 1819, A. D. du Loire-Atlantique, 3 J 26.
82. Powell, p.102.
83. Ris-Paquot, p.24.
84. *How to Improve the Condition of Domestic Service*, p.15.
85. Alq, pp.327-328; Pariset, pp.173 and 181; Parkes, p.122; Webster, p.328.
86. Pariset, p.81; household accounts of Count de Nantouillet, A. N., 154 A. P. V 41; accounts of a cultivator in the Landes, A. D. des Landes, F 968.
87. Baylis, p.8; Pariset, p.31; accounts of Madame Vermon, A. D. des Ardennes, 2 J 77 (10); Mary Abbot, *A Woman's Paris* (Boston, 1900), pp.30-31.
88. Pariset, pp.170-171; Webster, pp.325-326.
89. Hecht, pp.172-173; Ris-Paquot, p.26; Alq, p.186; Gustav Bienaymé, 'Le coût de la vie à Paris à diverses époques, Gages des domestiques', *Journal de la Société de Statistique de Paris*, XL (November, 1899), 97; *Domestic Servants as They are and as They ought to be. By a Practical Mistress of a Household* (Brighton, 1859), p.11-15; *The Servant's Practical Guide*, p.11.
90. Alq, p.186.

91. Burnett, p.226.
92. A.N., 107 A. P. 18, dossier 7.
93. A.N., 27 A.P. 17, dossier 3.
94. Statistique générale de la France, *Prix et Salaires à diverses époques* (Strasbourg, 1863), p.87.
95. Bienaymé, pp.366-385.
96. *Prix et Salaires,* pp.34-40.
97. *Ibid.*
98. Collet, p.23.
99. *Ibid.,* pp.14, 19, and 20.
100. *Ibid.,* p.13.
101. *Ibid.*
102. Hudry-Menos, p.416.
103. Butler, p.17; also in Miss Elizabeth Tytler, 'The Eternal Servant Problem', *The National Review,* LIII (March-August, 1909), 973. The thesis that wages played a large role in attracting servants into the occupation can be found in Layton, p.516.
104. Othenin Haussonville, 'La vie et les salaires à Paris', *Revue des Deux Mondes,* LVI (April, 1883), 834.
105. *Annuaire statistique de la France,* 1885, pp.284-285.
106. Wood, p.279.
107. Guy Routh, *Occupation and Pay in Great Britain, 1906-1960* (Cambridge, England, 1965), p.95.
108. Booth, VIII, p.222.
109. Collet, p.28.
110. Ivy Pinchbeck, *Women Workers and the Industrial Revolution, 1750-1850* (London, 1930), p.315.
111. Banks, pp.65-69.
112. Statistique générale de la France, *Bulletin de la Statistique generale,* II (1913).
113. This is the thesis of J. A. and Olive Banks, *Feminism and Family Planning in Victorian England* (New York, 1964); also see Chapter 7.
114. This increasing exclusivity of the middle-class nuclear family is the theme of Philippe Ariès, *Centuries of Childhood* (New York, 1962).
115. Membership in Parisian servant associations in 1911 constituted only 2.8 per cent of the total Parisian servant population, and the percentage for France as a whole was even lower.

CHAPTER 4

1. David Chaplin's research report for the U.S. Department of Labor, *Private Household Employment in the United States,* examined this important aspect of domestic service.
2. See Michael Anderson, *Family Structure in Nineteenth-Century Lancashire* (London, 1971), pp.152-155; also see Charles Tilly and C. Harold Brown, 'On Uprooting, Kinship, and the Auspices of Migration', *International Journal of Comparative Sociology,* VI, (1965), 139-164.
3. Seymour Martin Lipset and Reinhard Bendix, *Social Mobility in Industrial Society* (Berkeley, 1967), pp.213-226.
4. Papworth, p.106.
5. Booth, VIII, p.214.
6. See Chapter 2.
7. Office du Travail, *Le placement des employés, ouvriers, et domestiques en France, son histoire, son état actuel* (Paris, 1893), pp.458-463, hereinafter cited as 'Placement, 1893'; Office du Travail, *Seconde Enquête sur le*

placement des employés, des ouvriers, et des domestiques (Paris, 1901), pp.26-28, hereinafter cited as 'Placement, 1901'.

8. Placement, 1893, p.363.
9. Mittre, p.154.
10. A. N.,F⁷ 9817.
11. *How to Improve the Conditions of Domestic Service* (London, 1894), p.6.
12. Unemployment statistics are only calculated with difficulty since the supply of domestic labour was sometimes considered co-terminant with the female population; for example, the 1891 British census included among domestic servants many women who were helping out in their family homes.
13. Mittre, p.55; Cusenier, p.67; Mrs Lewis, *Domestic Service in the Present Day* (London, 1889), p.7.
14. Madeleine Auger, *Condition juridique et économique du personnel domestique féminin* (Paris, 1935), p.17.
15. See Figures in Chapter Three.
16. Henri Du Motey, *L'Esclavage à Rome. Le Servage au Moyen Age. La Domesticité dans les temps modernes* (Douai, 1881), p.252.
17. Pariset, pp.73, 174; Celnart, p.35; Parkes, p.131; *Book of Domestic Duties*, pp.16-17.
18. Alq, p.186.
19. *How to Improve the Conditions of Domestic Service*, p.16.
20. Celnart, p.32.
21. Margaret Powell, *Below Stairs* (London, 1968), pp.89-90.
22. Walsh, p.224; Mann, pp.29-30; Baylis, pp.12-17.
23. Rayner, p.49.
24. *How to Improve the Conditions of Domestic Service*, pp.10-11.
25. Parkes, p.27.
26. Parkyn, pp.147-150; Parliamentary Papers, 1903, I, bill no. 103.
27. Roué, p.87; Bouniceau-Gesmon, p.301; Belèze, p.385.
28. 'Cuisinier-philosophe', *Maîtres et domestiques fin-de-siècle* (Paris, 1898), p.36; Celnart, p.30.
29. Except for contemporary reports, the manuscript censuses are the only reliable source for this kind of analysis but they are difficult to use since they were taken only every five or ten years. Of the French censuses, 1872 and 1876 censuses are the most usable since they give the exact place of birth.
30. Versailles, Listes nominatives, 1866, 1872 and 1876, quartier du St. Louis.
31. Lyon, Listes nominatives, 1872 and 1876, 6ᵉ arrondissement.
32. Collet, p.25.
33. Collet concludes that the least efficient servants were gradually eliminated from the servant class, *ibid.*, p.28.
34. Thomas Hardy, *Far from the Madding Crowd* (New York, 1968).
35. A. Weber, *Les Usages Locaux* (Orléans, 1882), p.52.
36. Mittre, p.172; see the request for authorisation of open-air labour markets in Charente-Inférieure in 1842, A.N., F ⁷ 9817.
37. *Placement*, 1893, p.189; S. and S. Adams, p.31.
38. Parkes, p.151; Rayner, p.32.
39. Robert Marquant, 'Les bureaux de placement en France sous l'Empire et la Restauration', *Revue d' histoire économique et sociale*, XL (1962), 201.
40. Ivy Pinchbeck, *Women Workers and the Industrial Revolution, 1750-1850* (London, 1930), pp.16-19.
41. Richardson, pp.125-126.
42. Booth, VIII, p.226.
43. Board of Trade, Department of Labour Statistics, *Seventeenth Abstract of Labour Statistics*, pp.26-27.

44. *Placement,* 1893, pp.9-10.
45. Schmahl, p.190.
46. Mittre, p.238.
47. *Placement,* 1893, p.133.
48. Office du Travail, *Enquête sur le placement des employés, ouvriers, et domestiques à Paris, depuis la promulgation de la loi du 14 mars 1904* (Paris, 1909), p.148, hereinafter cited as Placement, 1909.
49. *Ibid.,* p.33.
50. *Placement,* 1893, pp.458-463.
51. *Placement,* 1901, pp.26-28.
52. Mirbeau, p.385.
53. *Almanach des mystères des bureaux et agences de placement* (Paris, n.d.), p.49; *Placement,* 1893, p.363 ff; Bouniceau-Gesmon, p.320.
54. Letter of Louise Romon, A. N., F 22 367.
55. Commission du Travail, 'Rapport', *Chambre des Députés, Rapports* (6th legis., special session, 1895, no.1677), p.2.
56. Richardson, p.8; *Domestic News,* April 1915, p.1.
57. *Le Serviteur* (1905-1912) and *Gazette des Cochers et des Gens de Maison* (1887-1910).
58. The only French women's magazine to run advertisements for servants was the feminist newspaper, *La Fronde* (1897-1905).
59. Cusenier, p.308 ff.
60. Pinchbeck, p.3.
61. See Chapter 2; Rowntree estimated that two-thirds of York's servants came from York, p.391.
62. *How to Improve the Conditions of Domestic Service,* p.6.
63. See Chapter 6.
64. Michael Anderson concluded for the families of Lancashire that 'clustering and co-residence obviously eased the migrant over the culture shock, such as it was', *Family Structure in Nineteenth-Century Lancashire* (Cambridge, 1971), p.155.

CHAPTER 5

1. John Burnett, ed., *The Annals of Labour: Autobiographies of British Working-Class People, 1820-1920* (Bloomington, Ind.,1974), p.221.
2. Paris, A.D. de Paris, D.Q. (Déclarations des Mutations par décès).
3. Emile de la Bedollière, *Les Industriels, Métiers et Professions en France* (Paris, 1842), p.48; Noriac, p.176; Karr, p.332.
4. Ronald-Henri Hubscher, 'Une contribution à la connaissance des milieux populaires ruraux au XIXᵉ siècle. Le livre de compte de la famille Flauhaut (1811-1877)', *Revue d'histoire économique et sociale,* XLVII, no.3 (1969), 392-393.
5. Rowntree, pp.112-113.
6. *Ibid.*
7. *Hints to Domestic Servants. By a Butler in a Gentleman's Family,* 2nd ed. (London, 1854), pp.110-111.
8. L. Broom and J. H. Smith, 'Bridging Occupations', *British Journal of Sociology,* XIV, no.4 (1963), 322.
9. Ephraim Harold Mizruchi, 'Alienation and Anomie: Theoretical and Empirical perspectives', *The New Sociology,* ed. Irving Horowitz (New York, 1964), p.256.
10. Alphonse de Lamartine, *Geneviève, Histoire d'une servante* (Paris, 1850).
11. Beaufreton, p.558; L.F. Fouin, *De l'état des domestiques en France et des moyens de les moraliser* (Paris, 1837), p.36; Parkes, p.132; Tytler, p.980.

12. Moll-Weiss, pp.199-200; R.-E. Chalamet, *Les Ouvriers Domestiques* (Paris, 1905), p.31; Bassinet, 'Avis présenté au nom de la Comission de surveillance et de perfectionnement de l'école professionnelle et de ménagère de jeunes filles', *Conseil municipal de Paris, Rapports,* no.36 (1893), pp.1-2; Louis Dausset, 'Proposition relative à la création d'un diplôme et d'un cours normal d'enseignement ménager', *Conseil municipal de Paris, Rapports,* no.15. (1904), *passim*; Kamm, pp.163-164; Campbell, p.238; Hewitt, p.78.

13. Dorothy Home McCall, 'Another Aspect of the Servant Problem', *The National Review,* LX (Sept. 1912-Feb. 1913), 970.

14. Baker, p.15; Pariset, p.24.

15. Baylis, p.4.

16. Willoughby de Broke, p.458.

17. Baylis, p.4.

18. Webster, p.341.

19. Maurice Garden, *Lyon et les Lyonnais au XIXe siècle* (Paris, 1971), pp.254-255.

20. Lyons, Listes nominatives, 1872, 2e arrondissement; the existence of this literacy data is due to the zeal of one census-taker who listed literacy (although it was not required) under the 'comments' section of the manuscript census for this district of 2,400 persons.

21. M. Fleury and P. Valmary, 'Le Progrès de l'instruction élémentaire de Louis XIV à Napoleon III d'après l'enquête de Louis Maggiolo (1877-1879)', *Population,* XII (1957), 87, chart no.12. Even though the departments which supplied Lyons with the greatest numbers of servants in 1872 had some of the highest levels of literacy in France, the level of servant literacy was still higher. Overall female literacy in the departments of Ain, Isère, Savoie, and Haute-Savoie averaged 70 to 79 per cent in 1872; the Saône-et-Loire, Loire, Drôme and Haute-Loire had female literacy rates of 60 to 69 per cent. Of the departments which supplied the most female servants, only the Rhône itself and Jura had overall female literacy rates of above 80 per cent, and these rates included in all cases both the higher urban literacy rates and the lower rural rates. Thus, the average literacy of servants in Lyons in 1872 was significant in terms of the rural areas from which servants were drawn.

22. *Statistique générale,* 1901, IV, 356.

23. *Ibid.,* p.511. This statement may be somewhat misleading. Naturally, servants would be more literate than the whole population since they were younger but even so, servants were significantly more literate than similar rural groups.

24. Theodore Zeldin, *France, 1848-1945* (Oxford, 1973), Vol. I, pp.18-19.

25. Letter of M. Souillet, *Le Serviteur,* April 29, 1908; letter of A.J., *Le Serviteur,* May 13, 1908; Edouard, p.34; Celnart, p.27; Willoughby de Broke, p.458.

26. Edouard, p.34; Digard, p.lxiii; Pariset, p.191; Willoughby de Broke, pp.458-459.

27. Versailles, A. D. des Yvelines, Série E, Actes de Mariage et Contrats de Mariage, 1825-1833, 1845-1853.

28. A study of the census records of the city of Amiens by R. Burr Litchfield, Brown University, has suggested that many servants returned to the countryside to marry, so that many may not have become assimilated into the urban population.

29. About one servant marriage in six in this period in Versailles was covered by a contract. This was not far from the overall average of marriages covered by contracts about one in five, but it does mean that this discussion pertains only to a minority of servants.

30. Hecht, p.19; Cadbury, p.48.

31. Statistique générale, *Statistique des Familles et des Habitations en 1911* (Paris, 1918), p.57 ff.

32. Lyon, Listes nominatives, 1872; the manuscript censuses did not generally list children who were residing away from their parents, and this may have exaggerated the situation with regard to servant families.

33. Versailles, Listes nominatives, 1872.

34. *Census of England and Wales*, 1851, manuscript census lists.

35. *Ibid.*, 1871.

36. See letter of servant Louis Lievin, *Journal des Gens de Maison,* April 8, 1892.

37. Mayhew, IV, p.258; *Why do Servants of the Nineteenth Century Dress as They Do?* (London, 1859), p.vi; Alq, pp.327-328; Pariset, pp.173, 181; Ris-Paquot, p.39.

38. Burnett, p.237.

39. *Ibid.*, p.191.

40. Adams, pp.24-25; annual reports of the Caisse d'Epargne à Paris from 1828 to 1914, A.N., 88 A. Q. 1-6, provide ample proof that servants were assiduous savers; see also the reports of the savings bank of Lyons in the Documents administratifs, Statistiques de Lyon, Archives municipales de Lyon, 1881 to 1897.

41. Paris, A.D. de.Paris, D.Q. 7 3417-3939 (1825), 3532-4022 (1853), 10.611-10.704 (1869), Déclarations des mutations par décès.

42. Panton, p.102; *Domestic Service. By an Old Servant* (London, 1917), p.99.

CHAPTER 6

1. Burnett, p.222.

2. Noriac, pp.176-177; Cusenier, p.234.

3. *Statistique générale*, 1896, IV, cxxii.

4. See, for example, Mrs Parkes, pp.117-119.

5. Belèze, p.368; *Du Louage des gens de service à gages* (Paris, 1902), p.13.

6. Leon Bizard and André Morin, *La Syphilis et les domestiques* (Paris, 1973), *passim.*

7. Walsh, p.223.

8. Butler, p.68; Cadbury, p.112; Black, p.216.

9. Papworth, p.108.

10. *Ibid.*, p.105.

11. *Ibid.*

12. Mann, p.12; Butler, p.64.

13. Butler, p.68.

14. J. Henri Lasalle, *Maison hospitalière. Project d'un établissement destiné à recevoir les femmes domestiques aux époques où elles sont sans place* (Paris, 1827), pp.9-10.

15. Juillerat, p.154.

16. 'Cuisinier-philosophe', p.16; Daubié, pp.86-87; Cretté-Breton, pp.232-233.

17. Pierre Chaunu, *La civilisation de l'Europe classique* (Paris, 1970), p.196; Alain Lottin, 'Naissances illégitimes et filles-mères à Lille au XVIIIe siècle', *Revue d'histoire moderne et contemporaine,* XVII (1970), p.321.

18. Lottin, pp.302, 312; Edward Shorter, 'Illegitimacy, Sexual Revolution, and Social Change in Modern Europe', *Journal of Interdisciplinary History,* II, no.2 (1971), p.250.

19. Mayhew, IV, p.257.

20. Lafabrègue, p.243.

21. *Ibid.*, p.251.

22.   Vincent, in *La Réforme sociale,* p.513.

23.   Mouillon, p.7.

24.   See Joan Scott and Louise Tilly, 'Women's Work and the Family in Nineteenth-Century Europe', *The Family in History,* ed. Charles Rosenberg (Philadelphia, 1975), pp.18-21.

25.   See Edward Shorter, 'Illegitimacy, Sexual Revolution and Social Change in Europe, 1750-1900', *Journal of Interdisciplinary History,* II (1971), 237-272, and 'Female Emancipation, Birth Control and Fertility in European History', 3rd ed.*American Journal Review,* LXXVIII (1973), 605-640.

26.   Dr Alexandre Parent-Duchatelet, *De la prostitution dans la ville de Paris* (Paris, 1857), p.74: P.O., Police Reports, 1916, V, 229; A.M. Royden, *et al., Downward Paths: An Inquiry into the Causes which Contribute to the Making of Prostitution* (London, 1916), p.15. However, some prostitutes may simply have listed themselves as servants to make themselves seem more respectable and to disguise their true occupation.

27.   Parent-Duchâtelet, p.94; Maxime Du Camp, *Paris, ses organes, ses fonctions, et sa vie, dans la seconde moitié du XIXe siècle,* 6 vols. (Paris, 1869-1875), III, p.429.

28.   Steven Marcus, The Other Victorians (New York, 1964), p.134.

29.   P.P., 1816, V, 229.

30.   Campbell, p.234; a similar statement in Hudry-Menos, p.410.

31.   This is the argument of Judith R. Walkowitz and Daniel J. Walkowitz in ' "We are not Beasts of the Field"; Prostitution and the Poor in Plymouth and Southampton under the Contagious Diseases Act', *Clio's Consciousness Raised,* eds. Mary S. Hartman and Lois Banner (New York 1974), pp.192-225.

32.   Parent-Duchatelet, p.93.

33.   *Ibid.,* p.74.

34.   *Ibid.,* p.100.

35.   Marcus, p.129.

36.   Royden, pp.15, 194.

37.   *Ibid.,* p.193.

38.   Butler, p.96.

39.   Réné Bouton, *L'infanticide, étude morale et juridique* (Paris, 1887), p.171; Ryckère, p.158 ff; Mittre, p.39.

40.   Ryckère, p.149; see discussion of illegitimacy above.

41.   Charles Pellarin, 'Maître et Servante', *L'Avenir des Femmes,* IX (December, 1877), 183.

42.   Cusenier, pp.276-277.

43.   Ryckère, p.351 ff.

44.   Lochhead, p.41.

45.   Parkes, p.117; Lewis, p.19; Celnart, p.16; Digard, p.L.

46.   Bouniceau-Gesmon, p.111.

47.   Mittre, p.73.

48.   Cusenier, p.220.

49.   *Gazette des Tribunaux,* June 27, 1885.

50.   *Archives d'anthropologie criminelle,* 3 vols (Paris, 1886-1888), I, p.421.

51.   Paris, *Recherches statistiques sur la ville de Paris et la departement de la Seine,* 4 vols. (Paris, 1821-1829), III (1826) and IV (1829), statistics on admittances to public hospitals; Lasalle, p.12; Hudry-Menos, p.411.

52.   In 1875, servants committed 4.5 per cent of the suicides in France, whereas they constituted 2.75 per cent of the population; in 1881, they committed 5 per cent of the suicides and constituted 3 per cent of the total population. *Annuaire statistique de la France,* 1875, p.97, and 1881, p.105.

53. Ellis, p.308.
54. P.P., 1834, XXXVI, Poor Law Reports, *passim*.
55. Burnett, pp.241-242.
56. Margaret Powell in *Below Stairs*.
57. Burnett, p.216.

CHAPTER 7

1. See Chapter 2, Tables 2.5 and 2.6.
2. Statistique générale de la France, *Statistique des Industries et des Professions*, 1896, pp.204, 296-297.
3. Parliamentary Papers, 1863, LIII, pt.I, 18.
4. The charwoman was not the only non-resident servant. Male servants who were married often lived out while filling the job of a live-in servant. Moreover, early in the twentieth century, there was a separate category in the English census for 'day workers', who were young single women for the most part. These women were distinguished from chars by the fact that they did not perform the heavy cleaning for which chars had traditionally been hired. 'Dailies', then, were simply non-resident servants who performed general domestic duties.
5. Papworth, p.108.
6. Retirement to the countryside by servants and other workers may have been the first kind of retirement for the lower classes, according to recent investigations of the aged in France of Professor Peter N. Stearns. For those servants with savings or a pension, a return to the country helped to stretch out the value of their savings and reunited them with friends or kin still residing there. But for those who had few resources and fewer friends left in the countryside, it must have been an uncomfortable and lonely existence.
7. See discussion of this topic in Chapter 3.
8. *Ibid.*
9. See Chapter 6 for examples of defiance.
10. See Branca, *Silent Sisterhood*.
11. Board of Trade, Department of Labour Statistics, *Seventeenth Abstract of Labour Statistics*, pp.314-315.
12. *Ibid.*
13. *Census of England and Wales*, 1901.
14. Broom and Smith, *passim*.
15. David Lockwood, *The Black-Coated Worker: A Study in Social Consciousness* (London, 1958).
16. Hufton, p.26.
17. Zeldin, pp.179-180.
18. Cadbury, p.111; Butler, p.73.
19. See Chapter 3.

CHAPTER 8

1. David Chaplin, 'Domestic Service and the Rationalisation of Household Economy', unpublished paper, November 1968.
2. See Branca, Chapter 3.
3. Both my sampling of London censuses and the work of Professor David Chaplin produced this average for London households.

4. Both England and Germany were more urbanised by 1900 than France.
5. Lucy Maynard Salmon, *Domestic Service,* 2nd ed. (New York, 1901), p.76.
6. *Ibid.,* pp.102-103.
7. Sidney and Beatrice Webb, *Industrial Democracy* (London, 1902), p.674; a footnote attributes to Beatrice Webb the argument that domestic service enjoyed a special bargaining advantage which allowed them to secure satisfactory wages which other female workers did not enjoy; W. T. Layton, 'Changes in the Wages of Domestic Servants during Fifty Years', *Journal of the Royal Statistical Society,* LXXI (1905), 515-524; Layton argued that domestic servants' wages increased so rapidly in the nineteenth century that they outdistanced English female workers' wages, but this argument is not clearly substantiated by available evidence.
8. *Annuaire statistique de la France,* LXVI (1961), 59.
9. *Census of England and Wales,* P.P., 1852-1853, LXXXVIII, part 1, cxli.
10. Richard Cobb in *The Police and the People,* p.235, uses prostitutes as indicators of feminine migration, pauperisation and certain types of female work patterns. How much better to use servanthood to convey a characteristic female work experience.

INDEX

63, 67, 115, 118, 121
Enfranchisement, 15
Etiquette, 21, 25
Etrennes, see perquisites
Exchange value for work, 9

Factory work for women, 47, 71
Family accounts, 64; see also individual families
Family life of servants, 56; contributions by servants, 82-83; parents' occupations, 92-93
Family limitation by servants, 84, 95
Far from the Madding Crowd, 75
Feminists, 23, 32
Feminisation of service, 9, 34, 39
Femme de confiance, 13
Femme de ménage, 13, 101; see also charwomen
Firing, 26, 27, 73, 100
First World War, 15, 111
Flaubert, Gustave, 31
Footmen, 11, 49, 56, 106
Freedom, lack of, 56, 67, 68, 108, 116

Galliffet, family accounts of, 59
Gatekeepers, 13
Geneviève, 84
Gifts, 58-60
Girls' Friendly Society, 77
Governesses, 12, 52
'Greatest plague of life', 19, 70

Hardy, Thomas, 75
Harrison, J.F.C., 10
Haussmann, Baron de, 51
Haute-Loire, 152
Haute-Savoie, 40-43, 152
Hiring, 27, 57-58, 70-81
Holidays, 55-56
Hospitals, use of, 103, 108
Hours of work, 55-56
Household size, 14, 19, 39, 117-118
Housekeepers, 12
Housemaids, 62, 75
Housing shortage, 51-52, 67

Illegitimacy, 26, 99, 102, 103, 104, 108
Illness, 53-54, 100, 108
Infanticide, 105-106, 107
Instructresses, 12
Intendants, 11
International Feminist Congress of 1900 (Paris), 23

Irish, 82
Isère, 152

Jarlin, Francoise, 87, 94, 97
Journals, servants', 79
July Monarchy, women's wages during, 47
Jura, 152

Kin, 46, 76-77, 82, 95, 108, 151
Kitchenmaids, 12, 95, 109
Kitchens, 52-53

Labour Department, survey of, 20
Ladies' companions, 13
Ladies' maids, 12, 52
Ladies of Providence, 77
Lamartine, Alphonse de, 84
Lanceley, William, 95
Latin America, 14, 116, 119
Lawyers, 21
Legal position, of employer, 24, 25-26; of servant, 15, 25-26
Leisure, 55-56
Le Play, Frédéric, 16
Literacy of servants, 84-87, 152
Live-in servants, decline of, 111-115
Livrets, 22
Lodgekeepers, 13
Lodgings of servants, 22, 50-54, 62, 67; value of, 62-63
Loire, 152
London, 14, 20, 22, 34, 36, 37, 45, 46, 52, 55, 62, 74, 86, 101, 104, 108, 112
Louis Napoleon, 77
Lower classes, 21-23, 55-56, 60, 62, 63-64, 68, 100, 102, 108
Luxembourg Commission of 1848, 25
Lyons, 18, 40, 44, 46, 49, 51, 52, 74, 85-86, 152

Madame Bovary, 31
Magistrates, 21
Maid of all work, 12, 20, 58, 60, 75
Male servants, 11-12, 15, 39, 50, 51, 60, 63, 83, 88, 155
Marriage, 68, 83, 84, 85, 87-95; spouses of servants, 87, 93-94
Maternity leave, 56
Hayhew, Henry, 22, 102
Merchants, wives of, 27
Metropolitan Association for Befriending Young Servants, M.A.B.Y.S., 77, 78